Supreme Ninja Foodi 2 Basket Air Fryer Cookbook UK

2333 Days Ninja Foodi 2 Basket Air Fryer Recipes Opening up a world of flavours without compromising your health

Carmen B. Zak

Copyright © 2023 by Carmen B. Zak- All rights reserved.

The content contained within this book may not be reproduced, duplicated, or transmitted without direct written permission from the author or the publisher. Under no circumstances will any blame or legal responsibility be held against the publisher, or author, for any damages, reparation, or monetary loss due to the information contained within this book, either directly or indirectly.

Legal Notice: This book is copyright protected. It is only for personal use. You cannot amend, distribute, sell, use, quote or paraphrase any part, or the content within this book, without the consent of the author or publisher.

Disclaimer Notice: Please note the information contained within this document is for educational and entertainment purposes only. All effort has been executed to present accurate, up to date, reliable, complete information. No warranties of any kind are declared or implied. Readers acknowledge that the author is not engaged in the rendering of legal, financial, medical, or professional advice. The content within this book has been derived from various sources. Please consult a licensed professional before attempting any techniques outlined in this book. By reading this document, the reader agrees that under no circumstances is the author responsible for any losses, direct or indirect, that are incurred as a result of the use of the information contained within this document, including, but not limited to, errors, omissions, or inaccuracies.

CONTENTS

Introduction: 9
Ninja Foodi 2 Basket Air Fryer Advantages 9
Ninja Foodi 2 Basket Air Fryer Usage Tips 9
Ninja Foodi 2 Basket Air Fryer Cleaning and Maintenance 10

Breakfast Recipes 11
Jelly Doughnuts 11
Morning Patties 11
Bacon And Egg Omelet 12
Wholemeal Blueberry Muffins 12
Breakfast Sammies 13
Asparagus And Bell Pepper Strata And Greek Bagels 14
French Toasts 15
Breakfast Meatballs 15
Cinnamon-raisin Bagels Everything Bagels 16
Quick And Easy Blueberry Muffins 17
Breakfast Sausage And Cauliflower 17
Potatoes Lyonnaise 18
Baked Peach Oatmeal 18
Breakfast Cheese Sandwich 19
Egg In Bread Hole 19
Blueberry Coffee Cake And Maple Sausage Patties 20
Sausage With Eggs 21
Savory Soufflé 21
Cheesy Baked Eggs 22
Puff Pastry 22
Onion Omelette And Buffalo Egg Cups 23

Snacks And Appetizers Recipes 24

Goat Cheese And Garlic Crostini & Sweet Bacon Potato Crunchies 24

Chicken Stuffed Mushrooms 25

Stuffed Bell Peppers 26

Veggie Shrimp Toast 26

Grill Cheese Sandwich 27

Fried Pickles 27

Crunchy Basil White Beans And Artichoke And Olive Pitta Flatbread 28

Crispy Calamari Rings 29

Crab Rangoon Dip With Crispy Wonton Strips 30

Mushroom Rolls 31

Jalapeño Popper Dip With Tortilla Chips 32

Pretzels 33

Chicken Crescent Wraps 34

Onion Pakoras 34

Waffle Fries 35

Cheddar Quiche 35

Garlic Bread 36

Pepperoni Pizza Dip 36

Jalapeño Poppers And Greek Potato Skins With Olives And Feta 37

Beef Jerky Pineapple Jerky 38

Air Fried Pot Stickers 38

Poultry Recipes 39

Pecan-crusted Chicken Tenders 39

Barbecue Chicken Drumsticks With Crispy Kale Chips 39

Crispy Fried Quail 40

Air Fried Chicken Legs 40

Broccoli And Cheese Stuffed Chicken 41

Chicken And Ham Meatballs With Dijon Sauce 41

Teriyaki Chicken Skewers 42

Garlic Dill Wings 42

Buttermilk Fried Chicken 43

Chicken With Pineapple And Peach 43

Crispy Sesame Chicken 44

Spicy Chicken Wings 45

Chicken Kebabs 45

Crisp Paprika Chicken Drumsticks And Chicken Breasts With Asparagus And Beans 46

Lemon-pepper Chicken Thighs With Buttery Roasted Radishes 47

Crispy Ranch Nuggets 48

Spicy Chicken Sandwiches With "fried" Pickles 49

Easy Chicken Thighs 50

Chili Chicken Wings 50

Asian Chicken 51

Chicken Ranch Wraps 51

Beef, Pork, And Lamb Recipes 52

Marinated Steak & Mushrooms 52

Yogurt Lamb Chops 52

Steak Fajitas With Onions And Peppers 53

Simple Lamb Meatballs 53

Cilantro Lime Steak 54

Kielbasa And Cabbage 54

Bell Peppers With Sausages 55

Asian Glazed Meatballs 55

Italian Sausages With Peppers And Teriyaki Rump Steak With Broccoli 56

Asian Pork Skewers 57

Honey Glazed Bbq Pork Ribs 57

Five-spice Pork Belly 58

Garlic Butter Steaks 58

Beef Kofta Kebab 59

Mozzarella Stuffed Beef And Pork Meatballs 59

　　Italian-style Meatballs With Garlicky Roasted Broccoli 60

　　Italian Sausage And Cheese Meatballs 61

　　Taco Seasoned Steak 61

　　Turkey And Beef Meatballs 62

　　Short Ribs & Root Vegetables 63

Fish And Seafood Recipes 63

　　Lemony Prawns And Courgette 63

　　Salmon Patties 64

　　Chilean Sea Bass With Olive Relish And Snapper With Tomato 65

　　Marinated Ginger Garlic Salmon 66

　　Blackened Red Snapper 66

　　Flavorful Salmon With Green Beans 67

　　Seasoned Tuna Steaks 67

　　Salmon With Broccoli And Cheese 68

　　Codfish With Herb Vinaigrette 68

　　Orange-mustard Glazed Salmon And Cucumber And Salmon Salad 69

　　Lemon Pepper Salmon With Asparagus 70

　　Coconut Cream Mackerel 70

　　Salmon Fritters With Courgette & Cajun And Lemon Pepper Cod 71

　　Fish Tacos 72

　　Steamed Cod With Garlic And Swiss Chard 73

　　Italian Baked Cod 73

　　Scallops And Spinach With Cream Sauce And Confetti Salmon Burgers 74

　　Prawns Curry 75

　　Honey Pecan Shrimp 75

　　Honey Teriyaki Salmon 76

Vegetables And Sides Recipes 76

Mushroom Roll-ups 76

Air-fried Tofu Cutlets With Cacio E Pepe Brussels Sprouts 77

Buffalo Seitan With Crispy Zucchini Noodles 78

Quinoa Patties 79

Balsamic-glazed Tofu With Roasted Butternut Squash 80

Bbq Corn 81

Garlic-rosemary Brussels Sprouts 81

Garlic Herbed Baked Potatoes 82

Balsamic Vegetables 82

Fresh Mix Veggies In Air Fryer 83

Garlic Potato Wedges In Air Fryer 83

Pepper Poppers 84

Zucchini With Stuffing 84

Lime Glazed Tofu 85

Breaded Summer Squash 85

Beets With Orange Gremolata And Goat's Cheese 86

Broccoli, Squash, & Pepper 86

Bacon Potato Patties 87

Rosemary Asparagus & Potatoes 87

Curly Fries 88

Desserts Recipes 88

Jelly Donuts 88

Crustless Peanut Butter Cheesecake And Pumpkin Pudding With Vanilla Wafers 89

Apple Crisp 90

Mini Blueberry Pies 90

Pineapple Wontons 91

Sweet Potato Donut Holes 91

Pumpkin Muffins 92

Victoria Sponge Cake 93

Olive Oil Cake & Old-fashioned Fudge Pie 94

Molten Chocolate Almond Cakes 95

Pecan And Cherry Stuffed Apples 95

Grilled Peaches 96

Brownies Muffins 96

Moist Chocolate Espresso Muffins 97

Zucchini Bread 97

Gluten-free Spice Cookies 98

Cinnamon Bread Twists 98

Cream Cheese Shortbread Cookies 99

Coconut-custard Pie And Pecan Brownies 99

Simple Pineapple Sticks And Crispy Pineapple Rings 100

Apple Wedges With Apricots And Coconut Mixed Berry Crisp 101

Recipe Index 102

Introduction:

In the realm of kitchen appliances, the Ninja Foodi 2 Basket Air Fryer stands tall as a culinary powerhouse, revolutionizing the way we cook and savor our favorite dishes. This advanced kitchen gadget seamlessly combines the efficiency of air frying with the convenience of dual baskets, presenting users with a versatile and time-saving solution for their everyday cooking needs.

Ninja Foodi 2 Basket Air Fryer Advantages

Dual Basket Efficiency: The standout feature of the Ninja Foodi 2 Basket Air Fryer lies in its dual basket design, allowing users to simultaneously cook different foods at varying temperatures and durations. This not only streamlines meal preparation but also ensures that each component of a dish is perfectly cooked, catering to the diverse preferences of households.

Multi-Functionality: Beyond air frying, the Ninja Foodi 2 Basket Air Fryer boasts a myriad of cooking functions, including roasting, baking, dehydrating, and broiling. This versatility eliminates the need for multiple appliances, making it a space-saving and cost-effective addition to any kitchen.

Rapid Air Circulation Technology: Equipped with advanced air circulation technology, this air fryer ensures consistent and efficient cooking by circulating hot air around the food. This not only results in a crispy exterior but also preserves the moisture within, producing succulent and flavorful dishes with less oil.

Large Capacity: With its spacious dual baskets, the Ninja Foodi 2 Basket Air Fryer caters to large families or social gatherings, making it an ideal choice for those who love entertaining. The generous capacity allows users to prepare generous portions without compromising on quality.

User-Friendly Controls: The intuitive control panel and easy-to-navigate settings make the Ninja Foodi 2 Basket Air Fryer accessible to users of all cooking skill levels. Pre-programmed functions, adjustable temperature, and timer settings ensure precise cooking, while the digital display provides real-time updates on the cooking process.

Ninja Foodi 2 Basket Air Fryer Usage Tips

Optimal Food Arrangement: To maximize the benefits of dual baskets, strategically arrange foods with similar cooking times and temperatures in each basket. This ensures uniform cooking and prevents overcooking or undercooking of individual components.

Preheating for Crispy Results: Preheating the Ninja Foodi 2 Basket Air Fryer before placing the food enhances crispiness. This step is especially crucial for achieving the desired texture when preparing items like french fries, chicken wings, or other crispy delights.

Layering for Efficient Cooking: When cooking different foods simultaneously, consider layering items within each basket to optimize space. Place smaller or thinner items on top, allowing for proper air circulation and preventing uneven cooking.

Utilizing Dehydrating Function: Explore the dehydrating function for preserving fruits, vegetables, or making homemade snacks. Adjust the temperature and time settings to achieve the desired level of dehydration, unlocking a new dimension of culinary creativity.

Experimenting with Marinades and Rubs: Enhance the flavor profile of your dishes by marinating or applying rubs to the ingredients before air frying. This not only infuses flavors but also contributes to a more appealing texture.

Rotating Baskets Midway: For dishes that require extended cooking times, consider rotating the baskets midway through the cooking process. This ensures even browning and guarantees that every part of the food receives the right amount of heat.

Monitoring and Adjusting Temperature: While the Ninja Foodi 2 Basket Air Fryer simplifies cooking with its pre-programmed functions, experienced users may find experimenting with temperature adjustments beneficial. This allows for customization based on personal preferences and specific recipes.

Ensuring Proper Airflow: To guarantee optimal air circulation, avoid overcrowding the baskets. Allow sufficient space between food items to ensure that hot air can circulate evenly, preventing uneven cooking.

Ninja Foodi 2 Basket Air Fryer Cleaning and Maintenance

Cooling Down Before Cleaning: Prioritize safety by allowing the Ninja Foodi 2 Basket Air Fryer to cool down before initiating the cleaning process. This prevents accidental burns and ensures a safer cleaning experience.

Dismantling for Thorough Cleaning: Take advantage of the air fryer's modular design by disassembling components for a more thorough cleaning. Remove the baskets, trays, and other removable parts to access all surfaces that may come into contact with food particles.

Hand Washing vs. Dishwasher: While many components of the Ninja Foodi 2 Basket Air Fryer are dishwasher safe, some users may prefer handwashing certain parts for a more gentle and controlled cleaning process. Refer to the user manual for specific guidelines on dishwasher compatibility.

Dealing with Stubborn Residue: Address stubborn residue or grease by soaking removable parts in warm, soapy water. For persistent stains, consider using a non-abrasive sponge or brush to gently scrub away residue without damaging the surfaces.

Cleaning the Heating Element: Regularly inspect and clean the heating element to ensure optimal performance. Use a damp cloth or sponge to wipe away any accumulated grease or food particles, taking care not to damage the sensitive components.

Emptying and Cleaning the Drip Tray: The drip tray plays a crucial role in collecting excess grease and debris. Empty and clean the drip tray regularly to prevent the buildup of residues, minimizing the risk of smoke and ensuring a healthier cooking environment.

Maintaining the Exterior: Extend the lifespan and aesthetic appeal of your Ninja Foodi 2 Basket Air Fryer by wiping down the exterior with a damp cloth. Avoid using abrasive cleaners or scouring pads that may scratch the surface.

Regular Maintenance Checks: Conduct routine maintenance checks to identify any signs of wear or malfunction. Inspect the power cord, control panel, and other components for any issues, and promptly address any concerns to ensure the longevity of the appliance.

Breakfast Recipes

Jelly Doughnuts

Servings: 4
Cooking Time: 6 Minutes

Ingredients:

- 1 package Pillsbury Grands
- ½ cup seedless raspberry jelly
- 1 tablespoon butter, melted
- ½ cup sugar

Directions:

1. Spread the Pillsbury dough and cut out 3 inches round doughnuts out of it.
2. Place the doughnuts in the air fryer baskets and brush them with butter.
3. Drizzle sugar over the doughnuts.
4. Return the air fryer basket 1 to Zone 1, and basket 2 to Zone 2 of the Ninja Foodi 2-Basket Air Fryer.
5. Choose the "Air Fry" mode for Zone 1 at 320 degrees F and 6 minutes of cooking time.
6. Select the "MATCH COOK" option to copy the settings for Zone 2.
7. Initiate cooking by pressing the START/PAUSE BUTTON.
8. Use a piping bag to inject raspberry jelly into each doughnut.
9. Serve.

Nutrition:

- (Per serving) Calories 102 | Fat 7.6g | Sodium 545mg | Carbs 1.5g | Fiber 0.4g | Sugar 0.7g | Protein 7.1g

Morning Patties

Servings: 4
Cooking Time: 13 Minutes.

Ingredients:

- 1 lb. minced pork
- 1 lb. minced turkey
- 2 teaspoons dry rubbed sage
- 2 teaspoons fennel seeds
- 2 teaspoons garlic powder
- 1 teaspoon paprika
- 1 teaspoon of sea salt
- 1 teaspoon dried thyme

Directions:

1. In a mixing bowl, add turkey and pork, then mix them together.
2. Mix sage, fennel, paprika, salt, thyme, and garlic powder in a small bowl.
3. Drizzle this mixture over the meat mixture and mix well.
4. Take 2 tablespoons of this mixture at a time and roll it into thick patties.
5. Place half of the patties in Zone 1, and the other half in Zone 2, then spray them all with cooking oil.
6. Return the crisper plate to the Ninja Foodi Dual Zone Air Fryer.
7. Choose the Air Fry mode for Zone 1 and set the temperature to 390 degrees F and the time to 13 minutes.
8. Select the "MATCH" button to copy the settings for Zone 2.
9. Initiate cooking by pressing the START/STOP button.
10. Flip the patties in the drawers once cooked halfway through.
11. Serve warm and fresh.

Nutrition:

- (Per serving) Calories 305 | Fat 25g | Sodium 532mg | Carbs 2.3g | Fiber 0.4g | Sugar 2g | Protein 18.3g

Bacon And Egg Omelet

Servings: 2
Cooking Time: 10
Ingredients:

- 2 eggs, whisked
- ½ teaspoon of chopped tomatoes
- Sea Salt and black pepper, to taste
- 2 teaspoons of almond milk
- 1 teaspoon of cilantro, chopped
- 1 small green chili, chopped
- 4 slices of bacon

Directions:
1. Take a bowl and whisk eggs in it.
2. Then add green chili salt, black pepper, cilantro, almond milk, and chopped tomatoes.
3. Oil greases the ramekins.
4. Pour this into ramekins.
5. Put the bacon in the zone 1 basket and ramekins in zone 2 basket of the Ninja Foodie 2-Basket Air Fryer.
6. Now for zone 1, set it to AIR FRY mode at 400 degrees F for 10 minutes
7. And for zone 2, set it 350 degrees for 10 minutes in AIR FRY mode.
8. Press the Smart finish button and press start, it will finish both at the same time.
9. Once done, serve and enjoy.

Nutrition:
- (Per serving) Calories 285| Fat 21.5g| Sodium1000 mg | Carbs 2.2g | Fiber 0.1g| Sugar1 g | Protein 19.7g

Wholemeal Blueberry Muffins

Servings: 6
Cooking Time: 15 Minutes
Ingredients:

- Olive oil cooking spray
- 120 ml unsweetened applesauce
- 60 ml honey
- 120 ml non-fat plain Greek yoghurt
- 1 teaspoon vanilla extract
- 1 large egg
- 350 ml plus 1 tablespoon wholemeal, divided
- ½ teaspoon baking soda
- ½ teaspoon baking powder
- ½ teaspoon salt
- 120 ml blueberries, fresh or frozen

Directions:
1. Lightly coat the inside of six silicone muffin cups or a six-cup muffin tin with olive oil cooking spray.
2. In a large bowl, combine the applesauce, honey, yoghurt, vanilla, and egg and mix until smooth. Sift in 350 ml of the flour, the baking soda, baking powder, and salt into the wet mixture, then stir until just combined. In a small bowl, toss the blueberries with the remaining 1 tablespoon flour, then fold the mixture into the muffin batter.
3. Divide the mixture evenly among the prepared muffin cups and place into the zone 1 drawer of the air fryer. Bake at 182°C for 12 to 15 minutes, or until golden brown on top and a toothpick inserted into the middle of one of the muffins comes out clean. Allow to cool for 5 minutes before serving.

Breakfast Sammies

Servings: 5
Cooking Time: 20 Minutes

Ingredients:

- Biscuits:
- 6 large egg whites
- 475 ml blanched almond flour, plus more if needed
- 1½ teaspoons baking powder
- ½ teaspoon fine sea salt
- 60 ml (½ stick) very cold unsalted butter (or lard for dairy-free), cut into ¼-inch pieces
- Eggs:
- 5 large eggs
- ½ teaspoon fine sea salt
- ¼ teaspoon ground black pepper
- 5 (30 g) slices Cheddar cheese (omit for dairy-free)
- 10 thin slices ham

Directions:

1. Spray the two air fryer drawers with avocado oil. Preheat the air fryer to 176°C. Grease two pie pans or two baking pans that will fit inside your air fryer. 2. Make the biscuits: In a medium-sized bowl, whip the egg whites with a hand mixer until very stiff. Set aside. 3. In a separate medium-sized bowl, stir together the almond flour, baking powder, and salt until well combined. Cut in the butter. Gently fold the flour mixture into the egg whites with a rubber spatula. If the dough is too wet to form into mounds, add a few tablespoons of almond flour until the dough holds together well. 4. Using a large spoon, divide the dough into 5 equal portions and drop them about 1 inch apart on one of the greased pie pans. Place the pan in the two air fryer drawers and bake for 11 to 14 minutes, until the biscuits are golden brown. Remove from the air fryer and set aside to cool. 5. Make the eggs: Set the air fryer to 192°C. Crack the eggs into the remaining greased pie pan and sprinkle with the salt and pepper. Place the eggs in the air fryer to bake for 5 minutes, or until they are cooked to your liking. 6. Open the air fryer and top each egg yolk with a slice of cheese . Bake for another minute, or until the cheese is melted. 7. Once the biscuits are cool, slice them in half lengthwise. Place 1 cooked egg topped with cheese and 2 slices of ham in each biscuit. 8. Store leftover biscuits, eggs, and ham in separate airtight containers in the fridge for up to 3 days. Reheat the biscuits and eggs on a baking sheet in a preheated 176°C air fryer for 5 minutes, or until warmed through.

Asparagus And Bell Pepper Strata And Greek Bagels

Servings: 6
Cooking Time: 14 To 20 Minutes

Ingredients:

- Asparagus and Bell Pepper Strata:
- 8 large asparagus spears, trimmed and cut into 2-inch pieces
- 80 ml shredded carrot
- 120 ml chopped red pepper
- 2 slices wholemeal bread, cut into ½-inch cubes
- 3 egg whites
- 1 egg
- 3 tablespoons 1% milk
- ½ teaspoon dried thyme
- Greek Bagels:
- 120 ml self-raising flour, plus more for dusting
- 120 ml plain Greek yoghurt
- 1 egg
- 1 tablespoon water
- 4 teaspoons sesame seeds or za'atar
- Cooking oil spray
- 1 tablespoon butter, melted

Directions:

1. Make the Asparagus and Bell Pepper Strata :
2. In a baking pan, combine the asparagus, carrot, red bell pepper, and 1 tablespoon of water. Bake in the air fryer at 166°C for 3 to 5 minutes, or until crisp-tender. Drain well.
3. Add the bread cubes to the vegetables and gently toss.
4. In a medium bowl, whisk the egg whites, egg, milk, and thyme until frothy.
5. Pour the egg mixture into the pan. Bake in the zone 1 drawer for 11 to 15 minutes, or until the strata is slightly puffy and set and the top starts to brown. Serve.
6. Make the Greek Bagels :
7. In a large bowl, using a wooden spoon, stir together the flour and yoghurt until a tacky dough forms. Transfer the dough to a lightly floured work surface and roll the dough into a ball.
8. Cut the dough into 2 pieces and roll each piece into a log. Form each log into a bagel shape, pinching the ends together.
9. In a small bowl, whisk the egg and water. Brush the egg wash on the bagels.
10. Sprinkle 2 teaspoons of the toppings on each bagel and gently press it into the dough.
11. Insert the crisper plate into the zone 2 drawer and the drawer into the unit. Preheat the drawer by selecting BAKE, setting the temperature to 166°C, and setting the time to 3 minutes. Select START/STOP to begin.
12. Once the drawer is preheated, spray the crisper plate with cooking spray. Drizzle the bagels with the butter and place them into the drawer.
13. Select BAKE, set the temperature to 166°C, and set the time to 10 minutes. Select START/STOP to begin.
14. When the cooking is complete, the bagels should be lightly golden on the outside. Serve warm.

French Toasts

Servings: 4
Cooking Time: 6 Minutes

Ingredients:
- 4 eggs
- 120g evaporated milk
- 6 tablespoons sugar
- 4 teaspoons olive oil
- ¼ teaspoon ground cinnamon
- ¼ teaspoon vanilla extract
- 8 bread slices

Directions:
1. Line each basket of "Zone 1" and "Zone 2" with a greased piece of foil.
2. Then Press your chosen zone - "Zone 1" or "Zone 2" and then rotate the knob to select "Air Fry".
3. Set the temperature to 200 degrees C and then set the time for 5 minutes to preheat.
4. In a large bowl, add all ingredients except for bread slices and beat until well combined.
5. Coat the bread slices with egg mixture evenly.
6. After preheating, arrange 4 bread slices into the basket of each zone.
7. Slide the basket into the Air Fryer and set the time for 6 minutes.
8. While cooking, flip the slices once halfway through.
9. After cooking time is completed, remove the French toasts from Air Fryer and serve warm.

Breakfast Meatballs

Servings: 18 Meatballs
Cooking Time: 15 Minutes

Ingredients:
- 450 g pork sausage meat, removed from casings
- ½ teaspoon salt
- ¼ teaspoon ground black pepper
- 120 ml shredded sharp Cheddar cheese
- 30 g cream cheese, softened
- 1 large egg, whisked

Directions:
1. Combine all ingredients in a large bowl. Form mixture into eighteen 1-inch meatballs.
2. Place meatballs into the two ungreased air fryer drawers. Adjust the temperature to 204°C and air fry for 15 minutes, shaking drawers three times during cooking. Meatballs will be browned on the outside and have an internal temperature of at least 64°C when completely cooked. Serve warm.

Cinnamon-raisin Bagels Everything Bagels

Servings: 4
Cooking Time: 14 Minutes

Ingredients:
- FOR THE BAGEL DOUGH
- 1 cup all-purpose flour, plus more for dusting
- 2 teaspoons baking powder
- 1 teaspoon kosher salt
- 1 cup reduced-fat plain Greek yogurt
- FOR THE CINNAMON-RAISIN BAGELS
- ¼ cup raisins
- ½ teaspoon ground cinnamon
- FOR THE EVERYTHING BAGELS
- ¼ teaspoon poppy seeds
- ¼ teaspoon sesame seeds
- ¼ teaspoon dried minced garlic
- ¼ teaspoon dried minced onion
- FOR THE EGG WASH
- 1 large egg
- 1 tablespoon water

Directions:

1. To prep the bagels: In a large bowl, combine the flour, baking powder, and salt. Stir in the yogurt to form a soft dough. Turn the dough out onto a lightly floured surface and knead five to six times, until it is smooth and elastic. Divide the dough in half.
2. Knead the raisins and cinnamon into one dough half. Leave the other dough half plain.
3. Divide both portions of dough in half to form a total of 4 balls of dough (2 cinnamon-raisin and 2 plain). Roll each ball of dough into a rope about 8 inches long. Shape each rope into a ring and pinch the ends to seal.
4. To prep the everything bagels: In a small bowl, mix together the poppy seeds, sesame seeds, garlic, and onion.
5. To prep the egg wash: In a second small bowl, beat together the egg and water. Brush the egg wash on top of each bagel.
6. Generously sprinkle the everything seasoning over the top of the 2 plain bagels.
7. To cook the bagels: Install a crisper plate in each of the two baskets. Place the cinnamon-raisin bagels in the Zone 1 basket and insert the basket in the unit. For best results, the bagels should not overlap in the basket. Place the everything bagels in the Zone 2 basket and insert the basket in the unit.
8. Select Zone 1, select AIR FRY, set the temperature to 325°F, and set the time to 14 minutes. Select MATCH COOK to match Zone 2 settings to Zone 1.
9. Press START/PAUSE to begin cooking.
10. When cooking is complete, use silicone-tipped tongs to transfer the bagels to a cutting board. Let cool for 2 to 3 minutes before cutting and serving.

Nutrition:
- (Per serving) Calories: 238; Total fat: 3g; Saturated fat: 1g; Carbohydrates: 43g; Fiber: 1.5g; Protein: 11g; Sodium: 321mg

Quick And Easy Blueberry Muffins

Servings: 8 Muffins
Cooking Time: 12 Minutes

Ingredients:
- 315 ml flour
- 120 ml sugar
- 2 teaspoons baking powder
- ¼ teaspoon salt
- 80 ml rapeseed oil
- 1 egg
- 120 ml milk
- 160 ml blueberries, fresh or frozen and thawed

Directions:
1. Preheat the air fryer to 165°C.
2. In a medium bowl, stir together flour, sugar, baking powder, and salt.
3. In a separate bowl, combine oil, egg, and milk and mix well.
4. Add egg mixture to dry ingredients and stir just until moistened.
5. Gently stir in the blueberries.
6. Spoon batter evenly into parchment paper-lined muffin cups.
7. Put the muffin cups in the two air fryer baskets and bake for 12 minutes or until tops spring back when touched lightly.
8. Serve immediately.

Breakfast Sausage And Cauliflower

Servings: 4
Cooking Time: 45 Minutes

Ingredients:
- 450 g sausage meat, cooked and crumbled
- 475 ml double/whipping cream
- 1 head cauliflower, chopped
- 235 ml grated Cheddar cheese, plus more for topping
- 8 eggs, beaten
- Salt and ground black pepper, to taste

Directions:
1. Preheat the air fryer to 176°C.
2. In a large bowl, mix the sausage, cream, chopped cauliflower, cheese and eggs. Sprinkle with salt and ground black pepper.
3. Pour the mixture into a greased casserole dish. Bake in the preheated air fryer for 45 minutes or until firm.
4. Top with more Cheddar cheese and serve.

Potatoes Lyonnaise

Servings: 4
Cooking Time: 31 Minutes
Ingredients:
- 1 sweet/mild onion, sliced
- 1 teaspoon butter, melted
- 1 teaspoon brown sugar
- 2 large white potatoes (about 450 g in total), sliced ½-inch thick
- 1 tablespoon vegetable oil
- Salt and freshly ground black pepper, to taste

Directions:
1. Preheat the air fryer to 188°C.
2. Toss the sliced onions, melted butter and brown sugar together in the zone 1 air fryer drawer. Air fry for 8 minutes, shaking the drawer occasionally to help the onions cook evenly.
3. While the onions are cooking, bring a saucepan of salted water to a boil on the stovetop. Par-cook the potatoes in boiling water for 3 minutes. Drain the potatoes and pat them dry with a clean kitchen towel.
4. Add the potatoes to the onions in the zone 1 air fryer drawer and drizzle with vegetable oil. Toss to coat the potatoes with the oil and season with salt and freshly ground black pepper.
5. Increase the air fryer temperature to 204°C and air fry for 20 minutes, tossing the vegetables a few times during the cooking time to help the potatoes brown evenly.
6. Season with salt and freshly ground black pepper and serve warm.

Baked Peach Oatmeal

Servings: 6
Cooking Time: 30 Minutes
Ingredients:
- Olive oil cooking spray
- 475 ml certified gluten-free rolled oats
- 475 ml unsweetened almond milk
- 60 ml honey, plus more for drizzling (optional)
- 120 ml non-fat plain Greek yoghurt
- 1 teaspoon vanilla extract
- ½ teaspoon ground cinnamon
- ¼ teaspoon salt
- 350 ml diced peaches, divided, plus more for serving (optional)

Directions:
1. Lightly coat the inside of a 6-inch cake pan with olive oil cooking spray. In a large bowl, mix together the oats, almond milk, honey, yoghurt, vanilla, cinnamon, and salt until well combined.
2. Fold in 180 ml peaches and then pour the mixture into the prepared cake pan. Sprinkle the remaining peaches across the top of the oatmeal mixture.
3. Place the cake pan into the zone 1 drawer and bake at 190°C for 30 minutes. Allow to set and cool for 5 minutes before serving with additional fresh fruit and honey for drizzling, if desired.

Breakfast Cheese Sandwich

Servings: 2
Cooking Time: 8 Minutes
Ingredients:
- 4 bread slices
- 2 provolone cheese slice
- ¼ tsp dried basil
- 2 tbsp mayonnaise
- 2 Monterey jack cheese slice
- 2 cheddar cheese slice
- ¼ tsp dried oregano

Directions:
1. In a small bowl, mix mayonnaise, basil, and oregano.
2. Spread mayonnaise on one side of the two bread slices.
3. Top two bread slices with cheddar cheese, provolone cheese, Monterey jack cheese slice, and cover with remaining bread slices.
4. Insert a crisper plate in the Ninja Foodi air fryer baskets.
5. Place sandwiches in both baskets.
6. Select zone 1, then select "air fry" mode and set the temperature to 390 degrees F for 8 minutes. Press "match" to match zone 2 settings to zone 1. Press "start/stop" to begin. Turn halfway through.

Nutrition:
- (Per serving) Calories 421 | Fat 30.7g |Sodium 796mg | Carbs 13.9g | Fiber 0.5g | Sugar 2.2g | Protein 22.5g

Egg In Bread Hole

Servings: 1
Cooking Time: 8 Minutes
Ingredients:
- 1 tablespoon butter, softened
- 2 eggs
- 2 slices of bread
- Salt and black pepper, to taste

Directions:
1. Line either basket of "Zone 1" and "Zone 2" with a greased piece of foil.
2. Press your chosen zone - "Zone 1" or "Zone 2" and then rotate the knob to select "Air Fryer".
3. Set the temperature to 160 degrees C, and then set the time for 3 minutes to preheat.
4. After preheating, place the butter on both sides of the bread. Cut a hole in the centre of the bread and crack the egg.
5. Slide the basket into the Air Fryer and set the time for 6 minutes.
6. After cooking time is completed, transfer the bread to a serving plate and serve.

Blueberry Coffee Cake And Maple Sausage Patties

Servings: 6
Cooking Time: 25 Minutes

Ingredients:
- FOR THE COFFEE CAKE
- 6 tablespoons unsalted butter, at room temperature, divided
- ⅓ cup granulated sugar
- 1 large egg
- 1 teaspoon vanilla extract
- ¼ cup packed light brown sugar
- ½ teaspoon ground cinnamon
- FOR THE SAUSAGE PATTIES
- ½ pound ground pork
- 2 tablespoons maple syrup
- ½ teaspoon dried sage
- ½ teaspoon dried thyme
- 1½ teaspoons kosher salt
- ½ teaspoon crushed fennel seeds
- ½ teaspoon red pepper flakes (optional)
- ¼ teaspoon freshly ground black pepper
- ¼ cup whole milk
- 1½ cups all-purpose flour, divided
- 1 teaspoon baking powder
- ¼ teaspoon salt
- 1 cup blueberries

Directions:
1. To prep the coffee cake: In a large bowl, cream together 4 tablespoons of butter with the granulated sugar. Beat in the egg, vanilla, and milk.
2. Stir in 1 cup of flour, along with the baking soda and salt, to form a thick batter. Fold in the blueberries.
3. In a second bowl, mix the remaining 2 tablespoons of butter, remaining ½ cup of flour, the brown sugar, and cinnamon to form a dry crumbly mixture.
4. To prep the sausage patties: In a large bowl, mix the pork, maple syrup, sage, thyme, salt, fennel seeds, red pepper flakes (if using), and black pepper until just combined.
5. Divide the mixture into 6 equal patties about ½ inch thick.
6. To cook the coffee cake and sausage patties: Spread the cake batter into the Zone 1 basket, top with the crumble mixture, and insert the basket in the unit. Install a crisper plate in the Zone 2 basket, add the sausage patties in a single layer, and insert the basket in the unit.
7. Select Zone 1, select BAKE, set the temperature to 350°F, and set the time to 25 minutes.
8. Select Zone 2, select AIR FRY, set the temperature to 375°F, and set the time to 12 minutes. Select SMART FINISH.
9. Press START/PAUSE to begin cooking.
10. When the Zone 2 timer reads 6 minutes, press START/PAUSE. Remove the basket and use silicone-tipped tongs to flip the sausage patties. Reinsert the basket and press START/PAUSE to resume cooking.
11. When cooking is complete, let the coffee cake cool for at least 5 minutes, then cut into 6 slices. Serve warm or at room temperature with the sausage patties.

Nutrition:
- (Per serving) Calories: 395; Total fat: 15g; Saturated fat: 8g; Carbohydrates: 53g; Fiber: 1.5g; Protein: 14g; Sodium: 187mg

Sausage With Eggs

Servings: 2
Cooking Time: 13
Ingredients:

- 4 sausage links, raw and uncooked
- 4 eggs, uncooked
- 1 tablespoon of green onion
- 2 tablespoons of chopped tomatoes
- Salt and black pepper, to taste
- 2 tablespoons of milk, dairy
- Oil spray, for greasing

Directions:
1. Take a bowl and whisk eggs in it.
2. Then pour milk, and add onions and tomatoes.
3. Whisk it all well.
4. Now season it with salt and black pepper.
5. Take one cake pan, that fit inside the air fryer and grease it with oil spray.
6. Pour the omelet in the greased cake pans.
7. Put the cake pan inside zone 1 air fryer basket of Ninja Foodie 2-Basket Air Fryer.
8. Now place the sausage link into the zone 2 basket.
9. Select bake for zone 1 basket and set the timer to 8-10 minutes at 300 degrees F.
10. For the zone 2 basket, select the AIR FRY button and set the timer to 12 minutes at 390 degrees.
11. Once the cooking cycle completes, serve by transferring it to plates.
12. Chop the sausage or cut it in round and then mix it with omelet.
13. Enjoy hot as a delicious breakfast.

Nutrition:
- (Per serving) Calories 240 | Fat 18.4g| Sodium 396mg | Carbs 2.8g | Fiber0.2g | Sugar 2g | Protein 15.6g

Savory Soufflé

Servings: 4
Cooking Time: 8 Minutes
Ingredients:

- 4 tablespoons light cream
- 4 eggs
- 2 tablespoons fresh parsley, chopped
- 2 fresh red chilies pepper, chopped
- Salt, as required

Directions:
1. In a bowl, add all the ingredients and beat until well combined.
2. Divide the mixture into 4 greased soufflé dishes.
3. Press either "Zone 1" and "Zone 2" of Ninja Foodi 2-Basket Air Fryer and then rotate the knob to select "Air Fry".
4. Set the temperature to 200 degrees C, and then set the time for 5 minutes to preheat.
5. After preheating, arrange soufflé dishes into the basket.
6. Slide basket into Air Fryer and set the time for 8 minutes.
7. After cooking time is completed, remove the soufflé dishes from Air Fryer and serve warm.

Cheesy Baked Eggs

Servings: 4
Cooking Time: 16 Minutes

Ingredients:
- 4 large eggs
- 57g smoked gouda, shredded
- Everything bagel seasoning, to taste
- Salt and pepper to taste

Directions:
1. Crack one egg in each ramekin.
2. Top the egg with bagel seasoning, black pepper, salt and gouda.
3. Place 2 ramekins in each air fryer basket.
4. Return the air fryer basket 1 to Zone 1, and basket 2 to Zone 2 of the Ninja Foodi 2-Basket Air Fryer.
5. Choose the "Air Fry" mode for Zone 1 and set the temperature to 400 degrees F and 16 minutes of cooking time.
6. Select the "MATCH COOK" option to copy the settings for Zone 2.
7. Initiate cooking by pressing the START/PAUSE BUTTON.
8. Serve warm.

Nutrition:
- (Per serving) Calories 190 | Fat 18g | Sodium 150mg | Carbs 0.6g | Fiber 0.4g | Sugar 0.4g | Protein 7.2g

Puff Pastry

Servings: 6
Cooking Time: 10 Minutes

Ingredients:
- 1 package (200g) cream cheese, softened
- 50g sugar
- 2 tablespoons plain flour
- ½ teaspoon vanilla extract
- 2 large egg yolks
- 1 tablespoon water
- 1 package frozen puff pastry, thawed
- 210g seedless raspberry jam

Directions:
1. Mix the cream cheese, sugar, flour, and vanilla extract until smooth, then add 1 egg yolk.
2. Combine the remaining egg yolk with the water. Unfold each sheet of puff pastry on a lightly floured board and roll into a 30 cm square. Cut into nine 10 cm squares.
3. Put 1 tablespoon cream cheese mixture and 1 rounded teaspoon jam on each. Bring 2 opposite corners of pastry over filling, sealing with yolk mixture.
4. Brush the remaining yolk mixture over the tops.
5. Press your chosen zone - "Zone 1" or "Zone 2" and then rotate the knob to select "Air Fry".
6. Set the temperature to 160 degrees C, and then set the time for 5 minutes to preheat.
7. After preheating, spray the Air-Fryer basket of each zone with cooking spray, line them with parchment paper, and place the pastry on them.
8. Slide the basket into the Air Fryer and set the time for 10 minutes.
9. After cooking time is completed, transfer them onto serving plates and serve.

Onion Omelette And Buffalo Egg Cups

Servings: 4
Cooking Time: 15 Minutes

Ingredients:
- Onion Omelette:
- 3 eggs
- Salt and ground black pepper, to taste
- ½ teaspoons soy sauce
- 1 large onion, chopped
- 2 tablespoons grated Cheddar cheese
- Cooking spray
- Buffalo Egg Cups:
- 4 large eggs
- 60 g full-fat cream cheese
- 2 tablespoons buffalo sauce
- 120 ml shredded sharp Cheddar cheese

Directions:
1. Make the Onion Omelette :
2. Preheat the zone 1 air fryer drawer to 180°C.
3. In a bowl, whisk together the eggs, salt, pepper, and soy sauce.
4. Spritz a small pan with cooking spray. Spread the chopped onion across the bottom of the pan, then transfer the pan to the zone 1 air fryer drawer.
5. Bake in the preheated air fryer for 6 minutes or until the onion is translucent.
6. Add the egg mixture on top of the onions to coat well. Add the cheese on top, then continue baking for another 6 minutes.
7. Allow to cool before serving.
8. Make the Buffalo Egg Cups :
9. Crack eggs into two ramekins.
10. In a small microwave-safe bowl, mix cream cheese, buffalo sauce, and Cheddar. Microwave for 20 seconds and then stir. Place a spoonful into each ramekin on top of the eggs.
11. Place ramekins into the zone 2 air fryer drawer.
12. Adjust the temperature to 160°C and bake for 15 minutes.
13. Serve warm.

Snacks And Appetizers Recipes
Goat Cheese And Garlic Crostini & Sweet Bacon Potato Crunchies

Servings: 8
Cooking Time: 7 Minutes

Ingredients:

- Goat Cheese and Garlic Crostini:
- 1 wholemeal baguette
- 60 ml olive oil
- 2 garlic cloves, minced
- 113 g goat cheese
- 2 tablespoons fresh basil, minced
- Sweet Bacon Potato Crunchies:
- 24 frozen potato crunchies
- 6 slices cooked bacon
- 2 tablespoons maple syrup
- 240 ml shredded Cheddar cheese

Directions:

1. Make the Goat Cheese and Garlic Crostini :
2. Preheat the air fryer to 190°C.
3. Cut the baguette into ½-inch-thick slices.
4. In a small bowl, mix together the olive oil and garlic, then brush it over one side of each slice of bread.
5. Place the olive-oil-coated bread in a single layer in the zone 1 air fryer basket and bake for 5 minutes.
6. Meanwhile, in a small bowl, mix together the goat cheese and basil.
7. Remove the toast from the air fryer, then spread a thin layer of the goat cheese mixture over the top of each piece and serve.
8. Make the Sweet Bacon Potato Crunchies :
9. Preheat the air fryer to 205°C.
10. Put the potato crunchies in the zone 2 air fryer basket. Air fry for 10 minutes, shaking the basket halfway through the cooking time.
11. Meanwhile, cut the bacon into 1-inch pieces.
12. Remove the potato crunchies from the air fryer basket and put into a baking pan. Top with the bacon and drizzle with the maple syrup. Air fry for 5 minutes, or until the crunchies and bacon are crisp.
13. Top with the cheese and air fry for 2 minutes, or until the cheese is melted.
14. Serve hot.

Chicken Stuffed Mushrooms

Servings: 6
Cooking Time: 15 Minutes.

Ingredients:

- 6 large fresh mushrooms, stems removed
- Stuffing:
- ½ cup chicken meat, cubed
- 1 (4 ounces) package cream cheese, softened
- ¼ lb. imitation crabmeat, flaked
- 1 cup butter
- 1 garlic clove, peeled and minced
- Black pepper and salt to taste
- Garlic powder to taste
- Crushed red pepper to taste

Directions:

1. Melt and heat butter in a skillet over medium heat.
2. Add chicken and sauté for 5 minutes.
3. Add in all the remaining ingredients for the stuffing.
4. Cook for 5 minutes, then turn off the heat.
5. Allow the mixture to cool. Stuff each mushroom with a tablespoon of this mixture.
6. Divide the stuffed mushrooms in the two crisper plates.
7. Return the crisper plate to the Ninja Foodi Dual Zone Air Fryer.
8. Choose the Air Fry mode for Zone 1 and set the temperature to 375 degrees F and the time to 15 minutes.
9. Select the "MATCH" button to copy the settings for Zone 2.
10. Initiate cooking by pressing the START/STOP button.
11. Serve warm.

Nutrition:

- (Per serving) Calories 180 | Fat 3.2g | Sodium 133mg | Carbs 32g | Fiber 1.1g | Sugar 1.8g | Protein 9g

Stuffed Bell Peppers

Servings:3
Cooking Time:16
Ingredients:
- 6 large bell peppers
- 1-1/2 cup cooked rice
- 2 cups cheddar cheese

Directions:
1. Cut the bell peppers in half lengthwise and remove all the seeds.
2. Fill the cavity of each bell pepper with cooked rice.
3. Divide the bell peppers amongst the two zones of the air fryer basket.
4. Set the time for zone 1 for 200 degrees for 10 minutes.
5. Select MATCH button of zone 2 basket.
6. Afterward, take out the baskets and sprinkle cheese on top.
7. Set the time for zone 1 for 200 degrees for 6 minutes.
8. Select MATCH button of zone 2 basket.
9. Once it's done, serve.

Nutrition:
- (Per serving) Calories 605| Fat 26g | Sodium477 mg | Carbs68.3 g | Fiber4 g| Sugar 12.5g | Protein25.6 g

Veggie Shrimp Toast

Servings: 4
Cooking Time: 3 To 6 Minutes
Ingredients:
- 8 large raw shrimp, peeled and finely chopped
- 1 egg white
- 2 garlic cloves, minced
- 3 tablespoons minced red pepper
- 1 medium celery stalk, minced
- 2 tablespoons cornflour
- ¼ teaspoon Chinese five-spice powder
- 3 slices firm thin-sliced no-salt wholemeal bread

Directions:
1. Preheat the air fryer to 175ºC.
2. In a small bowl, stir together the shrimp, egg white, garlic, red pepper, celery, cornflour, and five-spice powder. Top each slice of bread with one-third of the shrimp mixture, spreading it evenly to the edges. With a sharp knife, cut each slice of bread into 4 strips.
3. Place the shrimp toasts in the two air fryer baskets in a single layer. Air fry for 3 to 6 minutes, until crisp and golden brown.
4. Serve hot.

Grill Cheese Sandwich

Servings: 2
Cooking Time: 10

Ingredients:
- 4 slices of white bread slices
- 2 tablespoons of butter, melted
- 2 slices of sharp cheddar
- 2 slices of Swiss cheese
- 2 slices of mozzarella cheese

Directions:
1. Brush melted butter on one side of all the bread slices and then top the 2 bread slices with slices of cheddar, Swiss, and mozzarella, one slice per bread.
2. Top it with the other slice to make a sandwich.
3. Divide it between two baskets of the air fryer.
4. Turn on AIR FRY mode for zone 1 basket at 350 degrees F for 10 minutes.
5. Use the MATCH button for the second zone.
6. Once done, serve.

Nutrition:
- (Per serving) Calories 577 | Fat 38g | Sodium 1466mg | Carbs 30.5g | Fiber 1.1g | Sugar 6.5g | Protein 27.6g

Fried Pickles

Servings: 4
Cooking Time: 15 Minutes

Ingredients:
- 2 cups sliced dill pickles
- 1 cup flour
- 1 tablespoon garlic powder
- 1 tablespoon Cajun spice
- ½ tablespoon cayenne pepper
- Olive Oil or cooking spray

Directions:
1. Mix together the flour and spices in a bowl.
2. Coat the sliced pickles with the flour mixture.
3. Place a crisper plate in each drawer. Put the pickles in a single layer in each drawer. Insert the drawers into the unit.
4. Select zone 1, then AIR FRY, then set the temperature to 400 degrees F/ 200 degrees C with a 15-minute timer. To match zone 2 settings to zone 1, choose MATCH. To begin, select START/STOP.

Nutrition:
- (Per serving) Calories 161 | Fat 4.1g | Sodium 975mg | Carbs 27.5g | Fiber 2.2g | Sugar 1.5g | Protein 4g

Crunchy Basil White Beans And Artichoke And Olive Pitta Flatbread

Servings: 6
Cooking Time: 19 Minutes

Ingredients:

- Crunchy Basil White Beans:
- 1 (425 g) can cooked white beans
- 2 tablespoons olive oil
- 1 teaspoon fresh sage, chopped
- ¼ teaspoon garlic powder
- ¼ teaspoon salt, divided
- 1 teaspoon chopped fresh basil
- Artichoke and Olive Pitta Flatbread:
- 2 wholewheat pittas
- 2 tablespoons olive oil, divided
- 2 garlic cloves, minced
- ¼ teaspoon salt
- 120 ml canned artichoke hearts, sliced
- 60 ml Kalamata olives
- 60 ml shredded Parmesan
- 60 ml crumbled feta
- Chopped fresh parsley, for garnish (optional)

Directions:

1. Make the Crunchy Basil White Beans :
2. Preheat the air fryer to 190ºC.
3. In a medium bowl, mix together the beans, olive oil, sage, garlic, ⅛ teaspoon salt, and basil.
4. Pour the white beans into the air fryer and spread them out in a single layer.
5. Bake in zone 1 basket for 10 minutes. Stir and continue cooking for an additional 5 to 9 minutes, or until they reach your preferred level of crispiness.
6. Toss with the remaining ⅛ teaspoon salt before serving.
7. Make the Artichoke and Olive Pitta Flatbread :
8. Preheat the air fryer to 190ºC.
9. Brush each pitta with 1 tablespoon olive oil, then sprinkle the minced garlic and salt over the top.
10. Distribute the artichoke hearts, olives, and cheeses evenly between the two pittas, and place both into the zone 2 air fryer basket to bake for 10 minutes.
11. Remove the pittas and cut them into 4 pieces each before serving. Sprinkle parsley over the top, if desired.

Crispy Calamari Rings

Servings: 4
Cooking Time: 10 Minutes

Ingredients:
- 455g calamari rings, patted dry
- 3 tablespoons lemon juice
- 60g plain flour
- 1 teaspoon garlic powder
- 2 egg whites
- 60ml milk
- 220g panko breadcrumbs
- 1½ teaspoon salt
- 1½ teaspoon ground black pepper

Directions:
1. Allow the squid rings to marinade for at least 30 minutes in a bowl with lemon juice. Drain the water in a colander.
2. In a shallow bowl, combine the flour and garlic powder.
3. In a separate bowl, whisk together the egg whites and milk.
4. In a third bowl, combine the panko breadcrumbs, salt, and pepper.
5. Floured first the calamari rings, then dip in the egg mixture, and finally in the panko breadcrumb mixture.
6. Press either "Zone 1" or "Zone 2" and then rotate the knob to select "Air Fry".
7. Set the temperature to 200 degrees C, and then set the time for 5 minutes to preheat.
8. After preheating, spray the Air-Fryer basket with cooking spray and line with parchment paper. Arrange in a single layer and spritz them with cooking spray.
9. Slide the basket into the Air Fryer and set the time for 10 minutes.
10. After cooking time is completed, transfer them onto serving plates and serve.

Crab Rangoon Dip With Crispy Wonton Strips

Servings: 6
Cooking Time: 15 Minutes

Ingredients:
- FOR THE DIP
- 1 (6-ounce) can pink crab, drained
- 8 ounces (16 tablespoons) cream cheese, at room temperature
- ½ cup sour cream
- 1 tablespoon chopped scallions
- ½ teaspoon garlic powder
- 1 teaspoon Worcestershire sauce
- ¼ teaspoon kosher salt
- 1 cup shredded part-skim mozzarella cheese
- FOR THE WONTON STRIPS
- 12 wonton wrappers
- 1 tablespoon olive oil
- ¼ teaspoon kosher salt

Directions:
1. To prep the dip: In a medium bowl, mix the crab, cream cheese, sour cream, scallions, garlic powder, Worcestershire sauce, and salt until smooth.
2. To prep the wonton strips: Brush both sides of the wonton wrappers with the oil and sprinkle with salt. Cut the wonton wrappers into ¾-inch-wide strips.
3. To cook the dip and strips: Pour the dip into the Zone 1 basket, top with the mozzarella cheese, and insert the basket in the unit. Install a crisper plate in the Zone 2 basket, add the wonton strips, and insert the basket in the unit.
4. Select Zone 1, select BAKE, set the temperature to 330°F, and set the time to 15 minutes.
5. Select Zone 2, select AIR FRY, set the temperature to 350°F, and set the time to 6 minutes. Select SMART FINISH.
6. Press START/PAUSE to begin cooking.
7. When the Zone 2 timer reads 4 minutes, press START/PAUSE. Remove the basket and shake well to redistribute the wonton strips. Reinsert the basket and press START/PAUSE to resume cooking.
8. When the Zone 2 timer reads 2 minutes, press START/PAUSE. Remove the basket and shake well to redistribute the wonton strips. Reinsert the basket and press START/PAUSE to resume cooking.
9. When cooking is complete, the dip will be bubbling and golden brown on top and the wonton strips will be crunchy. Serve warm.

Nutrition:
- (Per serving) Calories: 315; Total fat: 23g; Saturated fat: 12g; Carbohydrates: 14g; Fiber: 0.5g; Protein: 14g; Sodium: 580mg

Mushroom Rolls

Servings: 10
Cooking Time: 10 Minutes

Ingredients:

- 2 tablespoons olive oil
- 200g large portobello mushrooms, finely chopped
- 1 teaspoon dried oregano
- ½ teaspoon crushed red pepper flakes
- ¼ teaspoon salt
- 200g cream cheese, softened
- 100g whole-milk ricotta cheese
- 10 flour tortillas
- Cooking spray

Directions:

1. Heat the oil in a frying pan over medium heat. Add the mushrooms and cook for 4 minutes.
2. Sauté until mushrooms are browned, about 4-6 minutes, with oregano, pepper flakes, and salt. Cool.
3. Combine the cheeses in a mixing bowl| fold the mushrooms until thoroughly combined. On the bottom centre of each tortilla, spread 3 tablespoons of the mushroom mixture. Tightly roll up and secure with toothpicks.
4. Press either "Zone 1" or "Zone 2" and then rotate the knob to select "Air Fry".
5. Set the temperature to 200 degrees C, and then set the time for 5 minutes to preheat.
6. After preheating, spray the basket with cooking spray and arrange rolls onto basket.
7. Slide the basket into the Air Fryer and set the time for 10 minutes.
8. After cooking time is completed, transfer them onto serving plates and serve.

Jalapeño Popper Dip With Tortilla Chips

Servings: 6
Cooking Time: 15 Minutes

Ingredients:
- FOR THE DIP
- 8 ounces cream cheese, at room temperature
- ½ cup sour cream
- 1 cup shredded Cheddar cheese
- ¼ cup shredded Parmesan cheese
- ¼ cup roughly chopped pickled jalapeños
- ½ teaspoon kosher salt
- ½ cup panko bread crumbs
- 2 tablespoons olive oil
- ½ teaspoon dried parsley
- FOR THE TORTILLA CHIPS
- 10 corn tortillas
- 2 tablespoons fresh lime juice
- 1 tablespoon olive oil
- ½ teaspoon kosher salt

Directions:
1. To prep the dip: In a medium bowl, mix the cream cheese, sour cream, Cheddar, Parmesan, jalapeños, and salt until smooth.
2. In a small bowl, combine the panko, olive oil, and parsley.
3. Pour the dip into a 14-ounce ramekin and top with the panko mixture.
4. To prep the chips: Brush both sides of each tortilla with lime juice, then with oil. Sprinkle with the salt. Using a sharp knife or a pizza cutter, cut each tortilla into 4 wedges.
5. To cook the dip and chips: Install a crisper plate in each of the two baskets. Place the ramekin of dip in the Zone 1 basket and insert the basket in the unit. Layer the tortillas in the Zone 2 basket and insert the basket in the unit.
6. Select Zone 1, select BAKE, set the temperature to 350°F, and set the time to 15 minutes.
7. Select Zone 2, select AIR FRY, set the temperature to 375°F, and set the time to 5 minutes. Select SMART FINISH.
8. Press START/PAUSE to begin cooking.
9. When the Zone 2 timer reads 3 minutes, press START/PAUSE. Remove the basket from the unit and give the basket a good shake to redistribute the chips. Reinsert the basket and press START/PAUSE to resume cooking.
10. When cooking is complete, the dip will be bubbling and golden brown and the chips will be crispy. Serve warm.

Nutrition:
- (Per serving) Calories: 406; Total fat: 31g; Saturated fat: 14g; Carbohydrates: 22g; Fiber: 1g; Protein: 11g; Sodium: 539mg

Pretzels

Servings: 8
Cooking Time: 6 Minutes

Ingredients:

- 360ml warm water
- 1 tablespoon dry active yeast
- 1 tablespoon sugar
- 1 tablespoon olive oil
- 500g plain flour
- 1 teaspoon salt
- 1 large egg
- 1 tablespoon water

Directions:

1. Combine warm water, yeast, sugar, and olive oil in a large mixing bowl. Stir everything together and leave aside for about 5 minutes.
2. Add 375g flour and a teaspoon of salt to the mixture. Stir well.
3. On a floured surface, roll out the dough. Knead for 3 to 5 minutes, or until the dough is no longer sticky, adding flour 1 tablespoon at a time if necessary.
4. The dough should be divided in half. At a time, work with half of the dough.
5. Each dough half should be divided into eight pieces.
6. Make a 45cm rope out of the dough. Make a U shape out of the dough. Twist the ends two more times.
7. Fold the ends of the dough over the spherical portion.
8. In a small mixing dish, whisk the egg and a tablespoon of water.
9. Brush the egg wash on both sides of the pretzel dough.
10. Press your chosen zone - "Zone 1" or "Zone 2" and then rotate the knob to select "Air Fryer".
11. Set the temperature to 185 degrees C, and then set the time for 5 minutes to preheat.
12. After preheating, arrange pretzels into the basket of each zone.
13. Slide the baskets into Air Fryer and set the time for 6 minutes.
14. After cooking time is completed, place on a wire rack for a few minutes, then transfer onto serving plates and serve.

Chicken Crescent Wraps

Servings: 6
Cooking Time: 12 Minutes.
Ingredients:
- 3 tablespoons chopped onion
- 3 garlic cloves, peeled and minced
- ¾ (8 ounces) package cream cheese
- 6 tablespoons butter
- 2 boneless chicken breasts, cubed, cooked
- 3 (10 ounces) cans refrigerated crescent roll dough

Directions:
1. Heat oil in a skillet and add onion and garlic to sauté until soft.
2. Add cooked chicken, sautéed veggies, butter, and cream cheese to a blender.
3. Blend well until smooth. Spread the crescent dough over a flat surface.
4. Slice the dough into 12 rectangles.
5. Spoon the chicken mixture at the center of each rectangle.
6. Roll the dough to wrap the mixture and form a ball.
7. Divide these balls into the two crisper plate.
8. Return the crisper plate to the Ninja Foodi Dual Zone Air Fryer.
9. Choose the Air Fry mode for Zone 1 and set the temperature to 390 degrees F and the time to 12 minutes.
10. Select the "MATCH" button to copy the settings for Zone 2.
11. Initiate cooking by pressing the START/STOP button.
12. Serve warm.

Nutrition:
- (Per serving) Calories 100 | Fat 2g |Sodium 480mg | Carbs 4g | Fiber 2g | Sugar 0g | Protein 18g

Onion Pakoras

Servings: 2
Cooking Time: 10 Minutes
Ingredients:
- 2 medium brown or white onions, sliced (475 ml)
- 120 ml chopped fresh coriander
- 2 tablespoons vegetable oil
- 1 tablespoon chickpea flour
- 1 tablespoon rice flour, or 2 tablespoons chickpea flour
- 1 teaspoon ground turmeric
- 1 teaspoon cumin seeds
- 1 teaspoon rock salt
- ½ teaspoon cayenne pepper
- Vegetable oil spray

Directions:
1. In a large bowl, combine the onions, coriander, oil, chickpea flour, rice flour, turmeric, cumin seeds, salt, and cayenne. Stir to combine. Cover and let stand for 30 minutes or up to overnight. Mix well before using.
2. Spray the air fryer baskets generously with vegetable oil spray. Drop the batter in 6 heaping tablespoons into the two baskets. Set the air fryer to 175°C for 8 minutes. Carefully turn the pakoras over and spray with oil spray. Set the air fryer for 2 minutes, or until the batter is cooked through and crisp, checking at 6 minutes for doneness. Serve hot.

Waffle Fries

Servings: 2
Cooking Time: 15 Minutes
Ingredients:
- 2 russet potatoes
- ½ teaspoon seasoning salt

Directions:
1. If desired, peel the potatoes.
2. With Wave-Waffle Cutter, slice potatoes by turning them one-quarter turn after each pass over the blade.
3. In a mixing dish, toss the potato pieces with the seasoning salt. Toss the potatoes in the seasoning to ensure that it is uniformly distributed.
4. Place a baking sheet on the baskets.
5. Press either "Zone 1" or "Zone 2" and then rotate the knob to select "Air Fryer".
6. Set the temperature to 200 degrees C, and then set the time for 5 minutes to preheat.
7. After preheating, arrange them into the basket.
8. Slide the basket into the Air Fryer and set the time for 15 minutes.
9. After cooking time is completed, place on a wire rack for a few minutes, then transfer onto serving plates and serve.

Cheddar Quiche

Servings: 2
Cooking Time: 12
Ingredients:
- 4 eggs, organic
- 1-1/4 cup heavy cream
- Salt, pinch
- ½ cup broccoli florets
- ½ cup cheddar cheese, shredded and for sprinkling

Directions:
1. Take a Pyrex pitcher and crack two eggs in it.
2. And fill it with heavy cream, about half the way up.
3. Add in the salt and then add in the broccoli and pour this into two quiche dishes, and top it with shredded cheddar cheese.
4. Now divide it between both zones of baskets.
5. For zone 1, set the time to 10-12 minutes at 325 degrees F.
6. Select the MATCH button for the zone 2 basket.
7. Once done, serve hot.

Nutrition:
- (Per serving) Calories 454| Fat40g | Sodium 406mg | Carbs 4.2g | Fiber 0.6g| Sugar1.3 g | Protein 20g

Garlic Bread

Servings: 8
Cooking Time: 10 Minutes

Ingredients:

- 60g butter, softened
- 3 tablespoons grated Parmesan cheese
- 2 garlic cloves, minced
- 2 teaspoons minced fresh parsley
- 8 slices of French bread

Directions:

1. Press either "Zone 1" or "Zone 2" and then rotate the knob to select "Bake".
2. Set the temperature to 175 degrees C, and then set the time for 5 minutes to preheat.
3. After preheating, combine the first four ingredients in a small mixing bowl| spread on bread. Arrange bread slices onto basket.
4. Slide the basket into the Air Fryer and set the time for 3 minutes.
5. After cooking time is completed, transfer them onto serving plates and serve.

Pepperoni Pizza Dip

Servings: 6
Cooking Time: 10 Minutes

Ingredients:

- 170 g soft white cheese
- 177 ml shredded Italian cheese blend
- 60 ml sour cream
- 1½ teaspoons dried Italian seasoning
- ¼ teaspoon garlic salt
- ¼ teaspoon onion powder
- 177 ml pizza sauce
- 120 ml sliced miniature pepperoni
- 60 ml sliced black olives
- 1 tablespoon thinly sliced green onion
- Cut-up raw vegetables, toasted baguette slices, pitta chips, or tortilla chips, for serving

Directions:

1. In a small bowl, combine the soft white cheese, 60 ml of the shredded cheese, the sour cream, Italian seasoning, garlic salt, and onion powder. Stir until smooth and the ingredients are well blended.
2. Spread the mixture in a baking pan. Top with the pizza sauce, spreading to the edges. Sprinkle with the remaining 120 ml shredded cheese. Arrange the pepperoni slices on top of the cheese. Top with the black olives and green onion.
3. Place the pan in the zone 1 air fryer basket. Set the air fryer to 175°C for 10 minutes, or until the pepperoni is beginning to brown on the edges and the cheese is bubbly and lightly browned.
4. Let stand for 5 minutes before serving with vegetables, toasted baguette slices, pitta chips, or tortilla chips.

Jalapeño Poppers And Greek Potato Skins With Olives And Feta

Servings: 8
Cooking Time: 45 Minutes

Ingredients:
- Jalapeño Poppers:
- Oil, for spraying
- 227 g soft white cheese
- 177 ml gluten-free breadcrumbs, divided
- 2 tablespoons chopped fresh parsley
- ½ teaspoon granulated garlic
- ½ teaspoon salt
- 10 jalapeño peppers, halved and seeded
- Greek Potato Skins with Olives and Feta:
- 2 russet or Maris Piper potatoes
- 3 tablespoons olive oil, divided, plus more for drizzling (optional)
- 1 teaspoon rock salt, divided
- ¼ teaspoon black pepper
- 2 tablespoons fresh coriander, chopped, plus more for serving
- 60 ml Kalamata olives, diced
- 60 ml crumbled feta
- Chopped fresh parsley, for garnish (optional)

Directions:
1. Make the Jalapeño Popper s: Line the zone 1 air fryer basket with parchment and spray lightly with oil. 2. In a medium bowl, mix together the soft white cheese, half of the breadcrumbs, the parsley, garlic, and salt. 3. Spoon the mixture into the jalapeño halves. Gently press the stuffed jalapeños in the remaining breadcrumbs. 4. Place the stuffed jalapeños in the prepared basket. 5. Air fry at 190°C for 20 minutes, or until the cheese is melted and the breadcrumbs are crisp and golden brown.
2. Make the Greek Potato Skins with Olives and Feta :
3. Preheat the air fryer to 190°C.
4. Using a fork, poke 2 to 3 holes in the potatoes, then coat each with about ½ tablespoon olive oil and ½ teaspoon salt.
5. Place the potatoes into the zone 2 air fryer basket and bake for 30 minutes.
6. Remove the potatoes from the air fryer, and slice in half. Using a spoon, scoop out the flesh of the potatoes, leaving a ½-inch layer of potato inside the skins, and set the skins aside.
7. In a medium bowl, combine the scooped potato middles with the remaining 2 tablespoons of olive oil, ½ teaspoon of salt, black pepper, and coriander. Mix until well combined.
8. Divide the potato filling into the now-empty potato skins, spreading it evenly over them. Top each potato with a tablespoon each of the olives and feta.
9. Place the loaded potato skins back into the air fryer and bake for 15 minutes.
10. Serve with additional chopped coriander or parsley and a drizzle of olive oil, if desired.

Beef Jerky Pineapple Jerky

Servings: 8
Cooking Time: 6 To 12 Hours
Ingredients:
- FOR THE BEEF JERKY
- ½ cup reduced-sodium soy sauce
- ¼ cup pineapple juice
- 1 tablespoon dark brown sugar
- 1 tablespoon Worcestershire sauce
- ½ teaspoon smoked paprika
- ¼ teaspoon freshly ground black pepper
- ¼ teaspoon red pepper flakes
- 1 pound beef bottom round, trimmed of excess fat, cut into ¼-inch-thick slices
- FOR THE PINEAPPLE JERKY
- 1 pound pineapple, cut into ⅛-inch-thick rounds, pat dry
- 1 teaspoon chili powder (optional)

Directions:
1. To prep the beef jerky: In a large zip-top bag, combine the soy sauce, pineapple juice, brown sugar, Worcestershire sauce, smoked paprika, black pepper, and red pepper flakes.
2. Add the beef slices, seal the bag, and toss to coat the meat in the marinade. Refrigerate overnight or for at least 8 hours.
3. Remove the beef slices and discard the marinade. Using a paper towel, pat the slices dry to remove excess marinade.
4. To prep the pineapple jerky: Sprinkle the pineapple with chili powder (if using).
5. To dehydrate the jerky: Arrange half of the beef slices in a single layer in the Zone 1 basket, making sure they do not overlap. Place a crisper plate on top of the beef slices and arrange the remaining slices in a single layer on top of the crisper plate. Insert the basket in the unit.
6. Repeat this process with the pineapple in the Zone 2 basket and insert the basket in the unit.
7. Select Zone 1, select DEHYDRATE, set the temperature to 150°F, and set the time to 8 hours.
8. Select Zone 2, select DEHYDRATE, set the temperature to 135°F, and set the time to 12 hours.
9. Press START/PAUSE to begin cooking.
10. When the Zone 1 timer reads 2 hours, press START/PAUSE. Remove the basket and check the beef jerky for doneness. If necessary, reinsert the basket and press START/PAUSE to resume cooking.

Nutrition:
- (Per serving) Calories: 171; Total fat: 6.5g; Saturated fat: 2g; Carbohydrates: 2g; Fiber: 0g; Protein: 25g; Sodium: 369mg

Air Fried Pot Stickers

Servings: 30 Pot Stickers
Cooking Time: 18 To 20 Minutes
Ingredients:
- 120 ml finely chopped cabbage
- 60 ml finely chopped red pepper
- 2 spring onions, finely chopped
- 1 egg, beaten
- 2 tablespoons cocktail sauce
- 2 teaspoons low-salt soy sauce
- 30 wonton wrappers
- 1 tablespoon water, for brushing the wrappers

Directions:
1. Preheat the air fryer to 180°C.
2. In a small bowl, combine the cabbage, pepper, spring onions, egg, cocktail sauce, and soy sauce, and mix well.
3. Put about 1 teaspoon of the mixture in the centre of each wonton wrapper. Fold the wrapper in half, covering the filling; dampen the edges with water, and seal. You can crimp the edges of the wrapper with your fingers, so they look like the pot stickers you get in restaurants. Brush them with water.
4. Place the pot stickers in the two air fryer baskets and air fry for 9 to 10 minutes, or until the pot stickers are hot and the bottoms are lightly browned.
5. Serve hot.

Poultry Recipes

Pecan-crusted Chicken Tenders

Servings: 4
Cooking Time: 12 Minutes

Ingredients:
- 2 tablespoons mayonnaise
- 1 teaspoon Dijon mustard
- 455 g boneless, skinless chicken tenders
- ½ teaspoon salt
- ¼ teaspoon ground black pepper
- 75 g chopped roasted pecans, finely ground

Directions:
1. In a small bowl, whisk mayonnaise and mustard until combined. Brush mixture onto chicken tenders on both sides, then sprinkle tenders with salt and pepper.
2. Place pecans in a medium bowl and press each tender into pecans to coat each side.
3. Place tenders into the two ungreased air fryer drawers in a single layer. Adjust the temperature to 190°C and roast for 12 minutes, turning tenders halfway through cooking. Tenders will be golden brown and have an internal temperature of at least 76°C when done. Serve warm.

Barbecue Chicken Drumsticks With Crispy Kale Chips

Servings: 4
Cooking Time: 20 Minutes

Ingredients:
- FOR THE DRUMSTICKS
- 1 tablespoon chili powder
- 2 teaspoons smoked paprika
- ¼ teaspoon kosher salt
- ¼ teaspoon garlic powder
- ¼ teaspoon freshly ground black pepper
- 2 teaspoons dark brown sugar
- 4 chicken drumsticks
- 1 cup barbecue sauce (your favorite)
- FOR THE KALE CHIPS
- 5 cups kale, stems and midribs removed, if needed
- ½ teaspoon garlic powder
- ½ teaspoon kosher salt
- ¼ teaspoon freshly ground black pepper

Directions:
1. To prep the drumsticks: In a small bowl, combine the chili powder, smoked paprika, salt, garlic powder, black pepper, and brown sugar. Rub the spice mixture all over the chicken.
2. To cook the chicken and kale chips: Install a crisper plate in each of the two baskets. Add the chicken drumsticks to the Zone 1 basket and insert the basket in the unit. Add the kale to the Zone 2 basket, sprinkle the kale with the garlic powder, salt, and black pepper and insert the basket in the unit.
3. Select Zone 1, select BAKE, set the temperature to 390°F, and set the time to 20 minutes.
4. Select Zone 2, select AIR FRY, set the temperature to 300°F, and set the time to 15 minutes. Select SMART FINISH.
5. Press START/PAUSE to begin cooking.
6. When the Zone 1 timer reads 5 minutes, press START/PAUSE. Remove the basket and brush the drumsticks with the barbecue sauce. Reinsert the basket and press START/PAUSE to resume cooking.
7. When cooking is complete, the chicken should be cooked through and the kale chips will be crispy. Serve hot.

Crispy Fried Quail

Servings: 8
Cooking Time: 6 Minutes
Ingredients:

- 8 boneless quail breasts
- 2 tablespoons Sichuan pepper dry rub mix
- ¾ cup rice flour
- ¼ cup all-purpose flour
- 2-3 cups peanut oil
- Garnish
- Sliced jalapenos
- Fresh lime wedges
- Fresh coriander

Directions:
1. Split the quail breasts in half.
2. Mix Sichuan mix with flours in a bowl.
3. Coat the quail breasts with flour mixture and place in the air fryer baskets.
4. Return the air fryer basket 1 to Zone 1, and basket 2 to Zone 2 of the Ninja Foodi 2-Basket Air Fryer.
5. Choose the "Air Fry" mode for Zone 1 at 300 degrees F and 6 minutes of cooking time.
6. Select the "MATCH COOK" option to copy the settings for Zone 2.
7. Initiate cooking by pressing the START/PAUSE BUTTON.
8. Flip the quail breasts once cooked halfway through.
9. Serve warm.

Nutrition:
- (Per serving) Calories 351 | Fat 11g |Sodium 150mg | Carbs 3.3g | Fiber 0.2g | Sugar 1g | Protein 33.2g

Air Fried Chicken Legs

Servings: 4
Cooking Time: 10 Minutes
Ingredients:

- 8 chicken legs
- 2 tablespoons olive oil
- 1 teaspoon salt
- 1 teaspoon black pepper
- 1 teaspoon smoked paprika
- 1 teaspoon garlic powder
- 1 teaspoon dried parsley

Directions:
1. Mix chicken with oil, herbs and spices in a bowl.
2. Divide the chicken legs in the air fryer baskets.
3. Return the air fryer basket 1 to Zone 1, and basket 2 to Zone 2 of the Ninja Foodi 2-Basket Air Fryer.
4. Choose the "Air Fry" mode for Zone 1 at 400 degrees F and 10 minutes of cooking time.
5. Select the "MATCH COOK" option to copy the settings for Zone 2.
6. Initiate cooking by pressing the START/PAUSE BUTTON.
7. Flip the chicken once cooked halfway through.
8. Serve warm.

Nutrition:
- (Per serving) Calories 220 | Fat 13g |Sodium 542mg | Carbs 0.9g | Fiber 0.3g | Sugar 0.2g | Protein 25.6g

Broccoli And Cheese Stuffed Chicken

Servings: 4
Cooking Time: 20 Minutes
Ingredients:
- 60 g cream cheese, softened
- 70 g chopped fresh broccoli, steamed
- 120 g shredded sharp Cheddar cheese
- 4 (170 g) boneless, skinless chicken breasts
- 2 tablespoons mayonnaise
- ¼ teaspoon salt
- ¼ teaspoon garlic powder
- ⅛ teaspoon ground black pepper

Directions:
1. In a medium bowl, combine cream cheese, broccoli, and Cheddar. Cut a 4-inch pocket into each chicken breast. Evenly divide mixture between chicken breasts; stuff the pocket of each chicken breast with the mixture.
2. Spread ¼ tablespoon mayonnaise per side of each chicken breast, then sprinkle both sides of breasts with salt, garlic powder, and pepper.
3. Place stuffed chicken breasts into the two ungreased air fryer drawers so that the open seams face up. Adjust the temperature to 180°C and air fry for 20 minutes, turning chicken halfway through cooking. When done, chicken will be golden and have an internal temperature of at least 76°C. Serve warm.

Chicken And Ham Meatballs With Dijon Sauce

Servings: 4
Cooking Time: 15 Minutes
Ingredients:
- Meatballs:
- 230 g ham, diced
- 230 g chicken mince
- 110 g grated Swiss cheese
- 1 large egg, beaten
- 3 cloves garlic, minced
- 15 g chopped onions
- 1½ teaspoons sea salt
- 1 teaspoon ground black pepper
- Cooking spray
- Dijon Sauce:
- 3 tablespoons Dijon mustard
- 2 tablespoons lemon juice
- 60 ml chicken broth, warmed
- ¾ teaspoon sea salt
- ¼ teaspoon ground black pepper
- Chopped fresh thyme leaves, for garnish

Directions:
1. Preheat the air fryer to 200°C. Spritz the two air fryer baskets with cooking spray.
2. Combine the ingredients for the meatballs in a large bowl. Stir to mix well, then shape the mixture in twelve 1½-inch meatballs.
3. Arrange the meatballs in a single layer in the two air fryer baskets. Air fry for 15 minutes or until lightly browned. Flip the balls halfway through.
4. Meanwhile, combine the ingredients, except for the thyme leaves, for the sauce in a small bowl. Stir to mix well.
5. Transfer the cooked meatballs on a large plate, then baste the sauce over. Garnish with thyme leaves and serve.

Teriyaki Chicken Skewers

Servings: 4
Cooking Time: 16 Minutes

Ingredients:

- 455g boneless chicken thighs, cubed
- 237ml teriyaki marinade
- 16 small wooden skewers
- Sesame seeds for rolling
- Teriyaki Marinade
- ⅓ cup soy sauce
- 59ml chicken broth
- ½ orange, juiced
- 2 tablespoons brown sugar
- 1 teaspoon ginger, grated
- 1 clove garlic, grated

Directions:

1. Blend teriyaki marinade ingredients in a blender.
2. Add chicken and its marinade to a Ziplock bag.
3. Seal this bag, shake it well and refrigerate for 30 minutes.
4. Thread the chicken on the wooden skewers.
5. Place these skewers in the air fryer baskets.
6. Return the air fryer basket 1 to Zone 1, and basket 2 to Zone 2 of the Ninja Foodi 2-Basket Air Fryer.
7. Choose the "Air Fry" mode for Zone 1 at 350 degrees F and 16 minutes of cooking time.
8. Select the "MATCH COOK" option to copy the settings for Zone 2.
9. Initiate cooking by pressing the START/PAUSE BUTTON.
10. Flip the skewers once cooked halfway through.
11. Garnish with sesame seeds.
12. Serve warm.

Nutrition:

- (Per serving) Calories 456 | Fat 16.4g | Sodium 1321mg | Carbs 19.2g | Fiber 2.2g | Sugar 4.2g | Protein 55.2g

Garlic Dill Wings

Servings: 4
Cooking Time: 25 Minutes

Ingredients:

- 900 g bone-in chicken wings, separated at joints
- ½ teaspoon salt
- ½ teaspoon ground black pepper
- ½ teaspoon onion powder
- ½ teaspoon garlic powder
- 1 teaspoon dried dill

Directions:

1. In a large bowl, toss wings with salt, pepper, onion powder, garlic powder, and dill until evenly coated. Place wings into the two ungreased air fryer drawers in a single layer.
2. Adjust the temperature to 200ºC and air fry for 25 minutes, shaking the drawer every 7 minutes during cooking. Wings should have an internal temperature of at least 76ºC and be golden brown when done. Serve warm.

Buttermilk Fried Chicken

Servings: 6
Cooking Time: 30 Minutes

Ingredients:

- 1½ pounds boneless, skinless chicken thighs
- 2 cups buttermilk
- 1 cup all-purpose flour
- 1 tablespoon seasoned salt
- ½ tablespoon ground black pepper
- 1 cup panko breadcrumbs
- Cooking spray

Directions:

1. Place the chicken thighs in a shallow baking dish. Cover with the buttermilk. Refrigerate for 4 hours or overnight.
2. In a large gallon-sized resealable bag, combine the flour, seasoned salt, and pepper.
3. Remove the chicken from the buttermilk but don't discard the mixture.
4. Add the chicken to the bag and shake well to coat.
5. Dip the thighs in the buttermilk again, then coat in the panko breadcrumbs.
6. Install a crisper plate in each drawer. Place half the chicken thighs in the zone 1 drawer and half in zone 2's, then insert the drawers into the unit.
7. Select zone 1, select AIR FRY, set temperature to 390 degrees F/ 200 degrees C, and set time to 30 minutes. Select MATCH to match zone 2 settings to zone 1. Press the START/STOP button to begin cooking.
8. When the time reaches 15 minutes, press START/STOP to pause the unit. Remove the drawers and flip the chicken. Re-insert the drawers into the unit and press START/STOP to resume cooking.
9. When cooking is complete, remove the chicken.

Nutrition:

- (Per serving) Calories 335 | Fat 12.8g | Sodium 687mg | Carbs 33.1g | Fiber 0.4g | Sugar 4g | Protein 24.5g

Chicken With Pineapple And Peach

Servings: 4
Cooking Time: 14 To 15 Minutes

Ingredients:

- 1 (450 g) low-sodium boneless, skinless chicken breasts, cut into 1-inch pieces
- 1 medium red onion, chopped
- 1 (230 g) can pineapple chunks, drained, 60 ml juice reserved
- 1 tablespoon peanut oil or safflower oil
- 1 peach, peeled, pitted, and cubed
- 1 tablespoon cornflour
- ½ teaspoon ground ginger
- ¼ teaspoon ground allspice
- Brown rice, cooked (optional)

Directions:

1. Preheat the air fryer to 195°C.
2. In a medium metal bowl, mix the chicken, red onion, pineapple, and peanut oil. Bake in the air fryer for 9 minutes. Remove and stir.
3. Add the peach and return the bowl to the air fryer. Bake for 3 minutes more. Remove and stir again.
4. In a small bowl, whisk the reserved pineapple juice, the cornflour, ginger, and allspice well. Add to the chicken mixture and stir to combine.
5. Bake for 2 to 3 minutes more, or until the chicken reaches an internal temperature of 75°C on a meat thermometer and the sauce is slightly thickened.
6. Serve immediately over hot cooked brown rice, if desired.

Crispy Sesame Chicken

Servings: 2
Cooking Time: 10 Minutes

Ingredients:

- 680g boneless chicken thighs, diced
- 2 tablespoons rice vinegar
- 1 tablespoon soy sauce
- 2 teaspoons minced fresh ginger
- 1 garlic clove, minced
- ¾ teaspoon salt
- ½ teaspoon black pepper
- 2 large eggs, beaten
- 1 cup cornstarch
- Sauce
- 59ml soy sauce
- 2 tablespoons rice vinegar
- ⅓ cup brown sugar
- 59ml water
- 1 tablespoon cornstarch
- 2 teaspoons sesame oil
- 2 tablespoons vegetable oil
- 2 garlic cloves, minced
- 2 teaspoons chile paste
- Garnish
- 1 tablespoon toasted sesame seeds

Directions:

1. Blend all the sauce ingredients in a saucepan and cook until it thickens then allow it to cool.
2. Mix chicken with black pepper, salt, garlic, ginger, vinegar, and soy sauce in a bowl.
3. Cover and marinate the chicken for 20 minutes.
4. Divide the chicken in the air fryer baskets.
5. Return the air fryer basket 1 to Zone 1, and basket 2 to Zone 2 of the Ninja Foodi 2-Basket Air Fryer.
6. Choose the "Air Fry" mode for Zone 1 and set the temperature to 400 degrees F and 10 minutes of cooking time.
7. Select the "MATCH COOK" option to copy the settings for Zone 2.
8. Initiate cooking by pressing the START/PAUSE BUTTON.
9. Pour the prepared sauce over the air fried chicken and drizzle sesame seeds on top.
10. Serve warm.

Nutrition:

- (Per serving) Calories 351 | Fat 16g |Sodium 777mg | Carbs 26g | Fiber 4g | Sugar 5g | Protein 28g

Spicy Chicken Wings

Servings: 8
Cooking Time: 30 Minutes
Ingredients:

- 900g chicken wings
- 1 tsp black pepper
- 12g brown sugar
- 1 tbsp chilli powder
- 57g butter, melted
- 1 tsp smoked paprika
- 1 tsp garlic powder
- 1 tsp salt

Directions:
1. In a bowl, toss chicken wings with remaining ingredients until well coated.
2. Insert a crisper plate in the Ninja Foodi air fryer baskets.
3. Add the chicken wings to both baskets.
4. Select zone 1, then select "air fry" mode and set the temperature to 355 degrees F for 30 minutes. Press "match" to match zone 2 settings to zone 1. Press "start/stop" to begin. Turn halfway through.

Nutrition:
- (Per serving) Calories 276 | Fat 14.4g |Sodium 439mg | Carbs 2.2g | Fiber 0.5g | Sugar 1.3g | Protein 33.1g

Chicken Kebabs

Servings: 4
Cooking Time: 9 Minutes
Ingredients:

- 455g boneless chicken breast, cut into 1-inch pieces
- 1 tablespoon avocado oil
- 1 tablespoon Tamari soy sauce
- 1 teaspoon garlic powder
- 1 teaspoon ground ginger
- 1 teaspoon chili powder
- 1 tablespoon honey
- 1 green capsicum, cut into 1-inch pieces
- 1 red capsicum, cut into 1-inch pieces
- 1 yellow capsicum, cut into 1-inch pieces
- 1 courgette, cut into 1-inch pieces
- 1 small red onion, cut into 1-inch pieces
- cooking spray

Directions:
1. Rub chicken with oil and place in a bowl.
2. Mix honey, chili powder, ginger, garlic and soy sauce in a bowl.
3. Pour this mixture over the chicken.
4. Cover and marinate the chicken for 15 minutes.
5. Thread the marinated chicken with veggies on wooden skewers alternately.
6. Divide the skewers and place in the air fryer baskets.
7. Return the air fryer basket 1 to Zone 1, and basket 2 to Zone 2 of the Ninja Foodi 2-Basket Air Fryer.
8. Choose the "Air Fry" mode for Zone 1 at 350 degrees F and 9 minutes of cooking time.
9. Select the "MATCH COOK" option to copy the settings for Zone 2.
10. Initiate cooking by pressing the START/PAUSE BUTTON.
11. Flip the skewers once cooked halfway through.
12. Serve warm.

Nutrition:
- (Per serving) Calories 546 | Fat 33.1g |Sodium 1201mg | Carbs 30g | Fiber 2.4g | Sugar 9.7g | Protein 32g

Crisp Paprika Chicken Drumsticks And Chicken Breasts With Asparagus And Beans

Servings: 4
Cooking Time: 25 Minutes

Ingredients:

- Crisp Paprika Chicken Drumsticks:
- 2 teaspoons paprika
- 1 teaspoon packed brown sugar
- 1 teaspoon garlic powder
- ½ teaspoon dry mustard
- ½ teaspoon salt
- Pinch pepper
- 1 garlic clove, minced
- 2 tablespoons extra-virgin olive oil, divided
- Salt and ground black pepper, to taste
- ½ red onion, sliced thinly
- 230 g asparagus, trimmed and cut into 1-inch lengths
- 2 (230 g) boneless, skinless chicken breasts, trimmed
- ¼ teaspoon paprika
- ½ teaspoon ground coriander
- 60 g baby rocket, rinsed and drained
- 4 (140 g) chicken drumsticks, trimmed
- 1 teaspoon vegetable oil
- 1 scallion, green part only, sliced thin on bias
- Chicken Breasts with Asparagus and Beans:
- 160 g canned cannellini beans, rinsed
- 1½ tablespoons red wine vinegar

Directions:

1. Make the Crisp Paprika Chicken Drumsticks :
2. Preheat the air fryer to 200ºC.
3. Combine paprika, sugar, garlic powder, mustard, salt, and pepper in a bowl. Pat drumsticks dry with paper towels. Using metal skewer, poke 10 to 15 holes in skin of each drumstick. Rub with oil and sprinkle evenly with spice mixture.
4. Arrange drumsticks in zone 1 air fryer basket, spaced evenly apart, alternating ends. Air fry until chicken is crisp and registers 90ºC, 22 to 25 minutes, flipping chicken halfway through cooking.
5. Transfer chicken to serving platter, tent loosely with aluminum foil, and let rest for 5 minutes. Sprinkle with scallion and serve.
6. Make the Chicken Breasts with Asparagus and Beans :
7. Preheat the air fryer to 200ºC.
8. Warm the beans in microwave for 1 minutes and combine with red wine vinegar, garlic, 1 tablespoon of olive oil, ¼ teaspoon of salt, and ¼ teaspoon of ground black pepper in a bowl. Stir to mix well.
9. Combine the onion with ⅛ teaspoon of salt, ⅛ teaspoon of ground black pepper, and 2 teaspoons of olive oil in a separate bowl. Toss to coat well.
10. Place the onion in the zone 2 air fryer basket and air fry for 2 minutes, then add the asparagus and air fry for 8 more minutes or until the asparagus is tender. Shake the basket halfway through. Transfer the onion and asparagus to the bowl with beans. Set aside.
11. Toss the chicken breasts with remaining ingredients, except for the baby rocket, in a large bowl.
12. Put the chicken breasts in the air fryer and air fry for 14 minutes or until the internal temperature of the chicken reaches at least 75ºC. Flip the breasts halfway through.
13. Remove the chicken from the air fryer and serve on an aluminum foil with asparagus, beans, onion, and rocket. Sprinkle with salt and ground black pepper. Toss to serve.

Lemon-pepper Chicken Thighs With Buttery Roasted Radishes

Servings: 4
Cooking Time: 28 Minutes

Ingredients:
- FOR THE CHICKEN
- 4 bone-in, skin-on chicken thighs (6 ounces each)
- 1 teaspoon olive oil
- 2 teaspoons lemon pepper
- ¼ teaspoon kosher salt
- FOR THE RADISHES
- 1 bunch radishes (greens removed), halved through the stem
- 1 teaspoon olive oil
- ¼ teaspoon kosher salt
- ¼ teaspoon freshly ground black pepper
- 1 tablespoon unsalted butter, cut into small pieces
- 2 tablespoons chopped fresh parsley

Directions:
1. To prep the chicken: Brush both sides of the chicken thighs with olive oil, then season with lemon pepper and salt.
2. To prep the radishes: In a large bowl, combine the radishes, olive oil, salt, and black pepper. Stir well to coat the radishes.
3. To cook the chicken and radishes: Install a crisper plate in each of the two baskets. Place the chicken skin-side up in the Zone 1 basket and insert the basket in the unit. Place the radishes in the Zone 2 basket and insert the basket in the unit.
4. Select Zone 1, select AIR FRY, set the temperature to 390°F, and set the time to 28 minutes.
5. Select Zone 2, select ROAST, set the temperature to 400°F, and set the time to 15 minutes. Select SMART FINISH.
6. Press START/PAUSE to begin cooking.
7. When the Zone 2 timer reads 5 minutes, press START/PAUSE. Remove the basket, scatter the butter pieces over the radishes, and reinsert the basket. Press START/PAUSE to resume cooking.
8. When cooking is complete, the chicken should be cooked through and the radishes will be soft. Stir the parsley into the radishes and serve.

Crispy Ranch Nuggets

Servings: 4
Cooking Time: 10 Minutes

Ingredients:
- 1 pound chicken tenders, cut into 1½–2-inch pieces
- 1 (1-ounce) sachet dry ranch salad dressing mix
- 2 tablespoons flour
- 1 egg
- 1 cup panko breadcrumbs
- Olive oil cooking spray

Directions:
1. Toss the chicken with the ranch seasoning in a large mixing bowl. Allow for 5–10 minutes of resting time.
2. Fill a resalable bag halfway with the flour.
3. Crack the egg into a small bowl and lightly beat it.
4. Spread the breadcrumbs onto a dish.
5. Toss the chicken in the bag to coat it. Dip the chicken in the egg mixture lightly, allowing excess to drain off. Roll the chicken pieces in the breadcrumbs, pressing them in, so they stick. Lightly spray with the cooking spray.
6. Install a crisper plate in both drawers. Place half the chicken tenders in the zone 1 drawer and half in the zone 2 one, then insert the drawers into the unit.
7. Select zone 1, select AIR FRY, set temperature to 390 degrees F/ 200 degrees C, and set time to 10 minutes. Select MATCH to match zone 2 settings to zone 1. Press the START/STOP button to begin cooking.
8. When the time reaches 6 minutes, press START/STOP to pause the unit. Remove the drawers and flip the chicken. Re-insert the drawers into the unit and press START/STOP to resume cooking.
9. When cooking is complete, remove the chicken.

Nutrition:
- (Per serving) Calories 244 | Fat 3.6g | Sodium 713mg | Carbs 25.3g | Fiber 0.1g | Sugar 0.1g | Protein 31g

Spicy Chicken Sandwiches With "fried" Pickles

Servings: 4
Cooking Time: 18 Minutes

Ingredients:
- FOR THE CHICKEN SANDWICHES
- 2 tablespoons all-purpose flour
- 2 large eggs
- 2 teaspoons Louisiana-style hot sauce
- 1 cup panko bread crumbs
- 1 teaspoon paprika
- ½ teaspoon garlic powder
- ¼ teaspoon salt
- ¼ teaspoon freshly ground black pepper
- ¼ teaspoon cayenne pepper (optional)
- 4 thin-sliced chicken cutlets (4 ounces each)
- 2 teaspoons vegetable oil
- 4 hamburger rolls
- FOR THE PICKLES
- 1 cup dill pickle chips, drained
- 1 large egg
- ½ cup panko bread crumbs
- Nonstick cooking spray
- ½ cup ranch dressing, for serving (optional)

Directions:
1. To prep the sandwiches:
2. Set up a breading station with three small shallow bowls. Place the flour in the first bowl. In the second bowl, whisk together the eggs and hot sauce. Combine the panko, paprika, garlic powder, salt, black pepper, and cayenne pepper in the third bowl.
3. Bread the chicken cutlets in this order: First, dip them into the flour, coating both sides. Then, dip into the egg mixture. Finally, coat them in the panko mixture, gently pressing the breading into the chicken to help it adhere. Drizzle the cutlets with the oil.
4. To prep the pickles:
5. Pat the pickles dry with a paper towel.
6. In a small shallow bowl, whisk the egg. Add the panko to a second shallow bowl.
7. Dip the pickles in the egg, then the panko. Mist both sides of the pickles with cooking spray.
8. To cook the chicken and pickles:
9. Install a crisper plate in each of the two baskets. Place the chicken in the Zone 1 basket and insert the basket in the unit. Place the pickles in the Zone 2 basket and insert the basket in the unit.
10. Select Zone 1, select AIR FRY, set the temperature to 390°F, and set the time to 18 minutes.
11. Select Zone 2, select AIR FRY, set the temperature to 400°F, and set the time to 15 minutes. Select SMART FINISH.
12. Press START/PAUSE to begin cooking.
13. When both timers read 10 minutes, press START/PAUSE. Remove the Zone 1 basket and use silicone-tipped tongs to flip the chicken. Reinsert the basket. Remove the Zone 2 basket and shake to redistribute the pickles. Reinsert the basket and press START/PAUSE to resume cooking.
14. When cooking is complete, the breading will be crisp and golden brown and the chicken cooked through. Place one chicken cutlet on each hamburger roll. Serve the "fried" pickles on the side with ranch dressing, if desired.

Easy Chicken Thighs

Servings: 8
Cooking Time: 12 Minutes

Ingredients:
- 900g chicken thighs, boneless & skinless
- 2 tsp chilli powder
- 2 tsp olive oil
- 1 tsp garlic powder
- 1 tsp ground cumin
- Pepper
- Salt

Directions:
1. In a bowl, mix chicken with remaining ingredients until well coated.
2. Insert a crisper plate in the Ninja Foodi air fryer baskets.
3. Place chicken thighs in both baskets.
4. Select zone 1 then select "air fry" mode and set the temperature to 390 degrees F for 12 minutes. Press "match" to match zone 2 settings to zone 1. Press "start/stop" to begin. Turn halfway through.

Nutrition:
- (Per serving) Calories 230 | Fat 9.7g | Sodium 124mg | Carbs 0.7g | Fiber 0.3g | Sugar 0.2g | Protein 33g

Chili Chicken Wings

Servings: 4
Cooking Time: 43 Minutes

Ingredients:
- 8 chicken wings drumettes
- cooking spray
- ⅛ cup low-fat buttermilk
- ¼ cup almond flour
- McCormick Chicken Seasoning to taste
- Thai Chili Marinade
- 1 ½ tablespoons low-sodium soy sauce
- ½ teaspoon ginger, minced
- 1 ½ garlic cloves
- 1 green onion
- ½ teaspoon rice wine vinegar
- ½ tablespoon Sriracha sauce
- ½ tablespoon sesame oil

Directions:
1. Put all the ingredients for the marinade in the blender and blend them for 1 minute.
2. Keep this marinade aside. Pat dry the washed chicken and place it in the Ziploc bag.
3. Add buttermilk, chicken seasoning, and zip the bag.
4. Shake the bag well, then refrigerator for 30 minutes for marination.
5. Remove the chicken drumettes from the marinade, then dredge them through dry flour.
6. Spread the drumettes in the two crisper plate and spray them with cooking oil.
7. Return the crisper plate to the Ninja Foodi Dual Zone Air Fryer.
8. Choose the Air Fry mode for Zone 1 and set the temperature to 390 degrees F and the time to 43 minutes
9. Select the "MATCH" button to copy the settings for Zone 2.
10. Initiate cooking by pressing the START/STOP button.
11. Toss the drumettes once cooked halfway through.
12. Now brush the chicken pieces with Thai chili sauce and then resume cooking.
13. Serve warm.

Asian Chicken

Servings: 4
Cooking Time: 12 Minutes

Ingredients:
- 8 chicken thighs, boneless
- 4 garlic cloves, minced
- 85g honey
- 120ml soy sauce
- 1 tsp dried oregano
- 2 tbsp parsley, chopped
- 1 tbsp ketchup

Directions:
1. Add chicken and remaining ingredients in a bowl and mix until well coated. Cover and place in the refrigerator for 6 hours.
2. Insert a crisper plate in the Ninja Foodi air fryer baskets.
3. Remove the chicken from the marinade and place them in both baskets.
4. Select zone 1 then select "air fry" mode and set the temperature to 390 degrees F for 12 minutes. Press "match" to match zone 2 settings to zone 1. Press "start/stop" to begin.

Nutrition:
- (Per serving) Calories 646 | Fat 21.7g | Sodium 2092mg | Carbs 22.2g | Fiber 0.6g | Sugar 18.9g | Protein 86.9g

Chicken Ranch Wraps

Servings: 4
Cooking Time: 22 Minutes

Ingredients:
- 1½ ounces breaded chicken breast tenders
- 4 (12-inch) whole-wheat tortilla wraps
- 2 heads romaine lettuce, chopped
- ½ cup shredded mozzarella cheese
- 4 tablespoons ranch dressing

Directions:
1. Place a crisper plate in each drawer. Place half of the chicken tenders in one drawer and half in the other. Insert the drawers into the unit.
2. Select zone 1, then AIR FRY, and set the temperature to 390 degrees F/ 200 degrees C with a 22-minute timer. To match zone 2 settings to zone 1, choose MATCH. To begin cooking, press the START/STOP button.
3. To pause the unit, press START/STOP when the timer reaches 11 minutes. Remove the drawers from the unit and flip the tenders over. To resume cooking, re-insert the drawers into the device and press START/STOP.
4. Remove the chicken from the drawers when they're done cooking and chop them up.
5. Divide the chopped chicken between warmed-up wraps. Top with some lettuce, cheese, and ranch dressing. Wrap and serve.

Nutrition:
- (Per serving) Calories 212 | Fat 7.8g | Sodium 567mg | Carbs 9.1g | Fiber 34.4g | Sugar 9.7g | Protein 10.6g

Beef, Pork, And Lamb Recipes

Marinated Steak & Mushrooms

Servings: 4
Cooking Time: 10 Minutes

Ingredients:

- 450g rib-eye steak, cut into ½-inch pieces
- 2 tsp dark soy sauce
- 2 tsp light soy sauce
- 15ml lime juice
- 15ml rice wine
- 15ml oyster sauce
- 1 tbsp garlic, chopped
- 8 mushrooms, sliced
- 2 tbsp ginger, grated
- 1 tsp cornstarch
- ¼ tsp pepper

Directions:

1. Add steak pieces, mushrooms, and the remaining ingredients to a zip-lock bag. Seal the bag and place it in the refrigerator for 2 hours.
2. Insert a crisper plate in the Ninja Foodi air fryer baskets.
3. Remove the steak pieces and mushrooms from the marinade and place them in both baskets.
4. Select zone 1, then select "air fry" mode and set the temperature to 380 degrees F for 10 minutes. Press "match" to match zone 2 settings to zone 1. Press "start/stop" to begin. Stir halfway through.

Yogurt Lamb Chops

Servings: 2
Cooking Time: 20

Ingredients:

- 1½ cups plain Greek yogurt
- 1 lemon, juice only
- 1 teaspoon ground cumin
- 1 teaspoon ground coriander
- ¾ teaspoon ground turmeric
- ¼ teaspoon ground allspice
- 10 rib lamb chops (1–1¼ inches thick cut)
- 2 tablespoons olive oil, divided

Directions:

1. Take a bowl and add lamb chop along with listed ingredients.
2. Rub the lamb chops well.
3. and let it marinate in the refrigerator for 1 hour.
4. Afterward takeout the lamb chops from the refrigerator.
5. Layer parchment paper on top of the baskets of the air fryer.
6. Divide it between ninja air fryer baskets.
7. Set the time for zone 1 to 20 minutes at 400 degrees F.
8. Select the MATCH button for the zone 2 basket.
9. Hit start and then wait for the chop to be cooked.
10. Once the cooking is done, the cool sign will appear on display.
11. Take out the lamb chops and let the chops serve on plates.

Nutrition:

- (Per serving) Calories1973 | Fat90 g| Sodium228 mg | Carbs 109.2g | Fiber 1g | Sugar 77.5g | Protein 184g

Steak Fajitas With Onions And Peppers

Servings: 6
Cooking Time: 15 Minutes
Ingredients:

- 1 pound steak
- 1 green bell pepper, sliced
- 1 yellow bell pepper, sliced
- 1 red bell pepper, sliced
- ½ cup sliced white onions
- 1 packet gluten-free fajita seasoning
- Olive oil spray

Directions:
1. Thinly slice the steak against the grain. These should be about ¼-inch slices.
2. Mix the steak with the peppers and onions.
3. Evenly coat with the fajita seasoning.
4. Install a crisper plate in both drawers. Place half the steak mixture in the zone 1 drawer and half in zone 2's, then insert the drawers into the unit.
5. Select zone 1, select AIR FRY, set temperature to 390 degrees F/ 200 degrees C, and set time to 15 minutes. Select MATCH to match zone 2 settings to zone 1. Press the START/STOP button to begin cooking.
6. When the time reaches 10 minutes, press START/STOP to pause the unit. Remove the drawers and flip the steak strips. Re-insert the drawers into the unit and press START/STOP to resume cooking.
7. Serve in warm tortillas.

Nutrition:
- (Per serving) Calories 305 | Fat 17g | Sodium 418mg | Carbs 15g | Fiber 2g | Sugar 4g | Protein 22g

Simple Lamb Meatballs

Servings: 4
Cooking Time: 15 Minutes
Ingredients:

- 1-pound ground lamb
- 1 teaspoon ground cinnamon
- 1 teaspoon ground cumin
- 2 teaspoons granulated onion
- 2 tablespoons fresh parsley
- Salt and black pepper, to taste

Directions:
1. Add ground lamb, onion, cinnamon, cumin, parsley, salt and pepper in a large bowl. Mix until well combined.
2. Make 1-inch balls from the mixture and set aside.
3. Grease each basket of "Zone 1" and "Zone 2" of Ninja Foodi 2-Basket Air Fryer.
4. Press "Zone 1" and "Zone 2" and then rotate the knob for each zone to select "Air Fry".
5. Set the temperature to 380 degrees F/ 195 degrees C for both zones and then set the time for 5 minutes to preheat.
6. After preheating, arrange the meatballs into the basket of each zone.
7. Slide each basket into Air Fryer and set the time for 12 minutes.
8. Flip the meatballs once halfway through.
9. Take out and serve warm.

Cilantro Lime Steak

Servings: 4
Cooking Time: 10 Minutes

Ingredients:
- 450g flank steak, sliced
- 1 tsp cumin
- 1 tsp olive oil
- 4 tsp soy sauce
- 12g cilantro, chopped
- ¼ tsp cayenne
- 45ml lime juice
- 2 tsp chilli powder
- ¼ tsp salt

Directions:
1. Add the sliced steak pieces and the remaining ingredients into a zip-lock bag. Seal the bag and place in the refrigerator for 2 hours.
2. Insert a crisper plate in the Ninja Foodi air fryer baskets.
3. Place the marinated steak pieces in both baskets.
4. Select zone 1, then select "air fry" mode and set the temperature to 380 degrees F for 10 minutes. Press "match" to match zone 2 settings to zone 1. Press "start/stop" to begin.

Kielbasa And Cabbage

Servings: 4
Cooking Time: 20 To 25 Minutes

Ingredients:
- 450 g smoked kielbasa sausage, sliced into ½-inch pieces
- 1 head cabbage, very coarsely chopped
- ½ brown onion, chopped
- 2 cloves garlic, chopped
- 2 tablespoons olive oil
- ½ teaspoon salt
- ½ teaspoon freshly ground black pepper
- 60 ml water

Directions:
1. Preheat the zone 1 air fryer drawer to 204°C.
2. In a large bowl, combine the sausage, cabbage, onion, garlic, olive oil, salt, and black pepper. Toss until thoroughly combined.
3. Transfer the mixture to the zone 1 drawer of the air fryer and pour the water over the top. Pausing two or three times during the cooking time to shake the drawer, air fry for 20 to 25 minutes, until the sausage is browned and the vegetables are tender.

Bell Peppers With Sausages

Servings: 4
Cooking Time: 20

Ingredients:
- 6 beef or pork Italian sausages
- 4 bell peppers, whole
- Oil spray, for greasing
- 2 cups of cooked rice
- 1 cup of sour cream

Directions:
1. Put the bell pepper in the zone 1 basket and sausages in the zone 2 basket of the air fryer.
2. Set zone 1 to AIR FRY MODE for 10 minutes at 400 degrees F.
3. For zone 2 set it to 20 minutes at 375 degrees F.
4. Hit the smart finish button, so both finish at the same time.
5. After 5 minutes take out the sausage basket and break or mince it with a plastic spatula.
6. Then, let the cooking cycle finish.
7. Once done serve the minced meat with bell peppers and serve over cooked rice with a dollop of sour cream.

Nutrition:
- (Per serving) Calories 1356 | Fat 81.2g | Sodium 3044 mg | Carbs 96g | Fiber 3.1g | Sugar 8.3g | Protein 57.2 g

Asian Glazed Meatballs

Servings: 4 To 6
Cooking Time: 10 Minutes

Ingredients:
- 1 large shallot, finely chopped
- 2 cloves garlic, minced
- 1 tablespoon grated fresh ginger
- 2 teaspoons fresh thyme, finely chopped
- 355 ml brown mushrooms, very finely chopped
- 2 tablespoons soy sauce
- Freshly ground black pepper, to taste
- 450 g beef mince
- 230 g pork mince
- 3 egg yolks
- 235 ml Thai sweet chili sauce (spring roll sauce)
- 60 ml toasted sesame seeds
- 2 spring onions, sliced

Directions:
1. Combine the shallot, garlic, ginger, thyme, mushrooms, soy sauce, freshly ground black pepper, beef and pork mince, and egg yolks in a bowl and mix the ingredients together. Gently shape the mixture into 24 balls, about the size of a golf ball.
2. Preheat the air fryer to 192ºC.
3. Air fry the meatballs in the two drawers for 8 minutes, turning the meatballs over halfway through the cooking time. Drizzle some of the Thai sweet chili sauce on top of each meatball and return the drawers to the air fryer, air frying for another 2 minutes. Reserve the remaining Thai sweet chili sauce for serving.
4. As soon as the meatballs are done, sprinkle with toasted sesame seeds and transfer them to a serving platter. Scatter the spring onions around and serve warm.

Italian Sausages With Peppers And Teriyaki Rump Steak With Broccoli

Servings: 7
Cooking Time: 28 Minutes

Ingredients:
- Italian Sausages with Peppers:
- 1 medium onion, thinly sliced
- 1 yellow or orange pepper, thinly sliced
- 1 red pepper, thinly sliced
- 60 ml avocado oil or melted coconut oil
- 1 teaspoon fine sea salt
- 6 Italian-seasoned sausages
- Dijon mustard, for serving (optional)
- Teriyaki Rump Steak with Broccoli:
- 230 g rump steak
- 80 ml teriyaki marinade
- 1½ teaspoons sesame oil
- ½ head broccoli, cut into florets
- 2 red peppers, sliced
- Fine sea salt and ground black pepper, to taste
- Cooking spray

Directions:
1. Make the Italian Sausages with Peppers :
2. Preheat the air fryer to 204°C.
3. Place the onion and peppers in a large bowl. Drizzle with the oil and toss well to coat the veggies. Season with the salt.
4. Place the onion and peppers in a pie pan and cook in the air fryer for 8 minutes, stirring halfway through. Remove from the air fryer and set aside.
5. Spray the zone 1 air fryer drawer with avocado oil. Place the sausages in the zone 1 air fryer drawer and air fry for 20 minutes, or until crispy and golden brown. During the last minute or two of cooking, add the onion and peppers to the drawer with the sausages to warm them through.
6. Place the onion and peppers on a serving platter and arrange the sausages on top. Serve Dijon mustard on the side, if desired.
7. Store leftovers in an airtight container in the fridge for up to 7 days or in the freezer for up to a month. Reheat in a preheated 200°C air fryer for 3 minutes, or until heated through.
8. Make the Teriyaki Rump Steak with Broccoli :
9. Toss the rump steak in a large bowl with teriyaki marinade. Wrap the bowl in plastic and refrigerate to marinate for at least an hour.
10. Preheat the air fryer to 204°C and spritz with cooking spray.
11. Discard the marinade and transfer the steak in the preheated zone 2 air fryer drawer. Spritz with cooking spray.
12. Air fry for 13 minutes or until well browned. Flip the steak halfway through.
13. Meanwhile, heat the sesame oil in a nonstick skillet over medium heat. Add the broccoli and red pepper. Sprinkle with salt and ground black pepper. Sauté for 5 minutes or until the broccoli is tender.
14. Transfer the air fried rump steak on a plate and top with the sautéed broccoli and pepper. Serve hot.

Asian Pork Skewers

Servings: 4
Cooking Time: 30 Minutes

Ingredients:

- 450g pork shoulder, sliced
- 30g ginger, peeled and crushed
- ½ tablespoon crushed garlic
- 67½ml soy sauce
- 22½ml honey
- 22½ml rice vinegar
- 10ml toasted sesame oil
- 8 skewers

Directions:

1. Pound the pork slices with a mallet.
2. Mix ginger, garlic, soy sauce, honey, rice vinegar, and sesame oil in a bowl.
3. Add pork slices to the marinade and mix well to coat.
4. Cover and marinate the pork for 30 minutes.
5. Thread the pork on the wooden skewers and place them in the air fryer baskets.
6. Return the air fryer basket 1 to Zone 1, and basket 2 to Zone 2 of the Ninja Foodi 2-Basket Air Fryer.
7. Choose the "Air Fry" mode for Zone 1 and set the temperature to 350 degrees F and 25 minutes of cooking time.
8. Select the "MATCH COOK" option to copy the settings for Zone 2.
9. Initiate cooking by pressing the START/PAUSE BUTTON.
10. Flip the skewers once cooked halfway through.
11. Serve warm.

Honey Glazed Bbq Pork Ribs

Servings: 4
Cooking Time: 30 Minutes

Ingredients:

- 2 pounds pork ribs
- ¼ cup honey, divided
- 1 cup BBQ sauce
- ½ teaspoon garlic powder
- 2 tablespoons tomato ketchup
- 1 tablespoon Worcestershire sauce
- 1 tablespoon low-sodium soy sauce
- Freshly ground white pepper, as required

Directions:

1. In a bowl, mix together honey and the remaining ingredients except pork ribs.
2. Add the pork ribs and coat with the mixture generously.
3. Refrigerate to marinate for about 20 minutes.
4. Grease each basket of "Zone 1" and "Zone 2" of Ninja Foodi 2-Basket Air Fryer.
5. Press "Zone 1" and "Zone 2" and then rotate the knob for each zone to select "Air Fry".
6. Set the temperature to 355 degrees F/ 180 degrees C for both zones and then set the time for 5 minutes to preheat.
7. After preheating, arrange the ribs into the basket of each zone.
8. Slide each basket into Air Fryer and set the time for 26 minutes.
9. While cooking, flip the ribs once halfway through.
10. After cooking time is completed, remove the ribs from Air Fryer and place onto serving plates.
11. Drizzle with the remaining honey and serve immediately.

Five-spice Pork Belly

Servings: 4
Cooking Time: 17 Minutes
Ingredients:

- 450 g unsalted pork belly
- 2 teaspoons Chinese five-spice powder
- Sauce:
- 1 tablespoon coconut oil
- 1 (1-inch) piece fresh ginger, peeled and grated
- 2 cloves garlic, minced
- 120 ml beef or chicken stock
- ¼ to 120 ml liquid or powdered sweetener
- 3 tablespoons wheat-free tamari
- 1 spring onion, sliced, plus more for garnish

Directions:
1. Spray the two air fryer drawers with avocado oil. Preheat the air fryer to 204°C. 2. Cut the pork belly into ½-inch-thick slices and season well on all sides with the five-spice powder. Place the slices in a single layer in the two air fryer drawers and cook for 8 minutes, or until cooked to your liking, flipping halfway through. 3. While the pork belly cooks, make the sauce: Heat the coconut oil in a small saucepan over medium heat. Add the ginger and garlic and sauté for 1 minute, or until fragrant. Add the stock, sweetener, and tamari and simmer for 10 to 15 minutes, until thickened. Add the spring onion and cook for another minute, until the spring onion is softened. Taste and adjust the seasoning to your liking. 4. Transfer the pork belly to a large bowl. Pour the sauce over the pork belly and coat well. Place the pork belly slices on a serving platter and garnish with sliced spring onions. 5. Best served fresh. Store leftovers in an airtight container in the fridge for up to 4 days. Reheat in a preheated 204°C air fryer for 3 minutes, or until heated through.

Garlic Butter Steaks

Servings: 2
Cooking Time: 25 Minutes
Ingredients:

- 2 (6 ounces each) sirloin steaks or ribeyes
- 2 tablespoons unsalted butter
- 1 clove garlic, crushed
- ½ teaspoon dried parsley
- ½ teaspoon dried rosemary
- Salt and pepper, to taste

Directions:
1. Season the steaks with salt and pepper and set them to rest for about 2 hours before cooking.
2. Put the butter in a bowl. Add the garlic, parsley, and rosemary. Allow the butter to soften.
3. Whip together with a fork or spoon once the butter has softened.
4. When you're ready to cook, install a crisper plate in both drawers. Place the sirloin steaks in a single layer in each drawer. Insert the drawers into the unit.
5. Select zone 1, select AIR FRY, set temperature to 360 degrees F/ 180 degrees C, and set time to 10 minutes. Select MATCH to match zone 2 settings to zone 1. Select START/STOP to begin.
6. Once done, serve with the garlic butter.

Nutrition:
- (Per serving) Calories 519 | Fat 36g | Sodium 245mg | Carbs 1g | Fiber 0g | Sugar 0g | Protein 46g

Beef Kofta Kebab

Servings: 4
Cooking Time: 20 Minutes

Ingredients:

- 455g ground beef
- ¼ cup white onion, grated
- ¼ cup parsley, chopped
- 1 tablespoon mint, chopped
- 2 cloves garlic, minced
- 1 teaspoon salt
- ½ teaspoon cumin
- 1 teaspoon oregano
- ½ teaspoon garlic salt
- 1 egg

Directions:

1. Mix ground beef with onion, parsley, mint, garlic, cumin, oregano, garlic salt and egg in a bowl.
2. Take 3 tbsp-sized beef kebabs out of this mixture.
3. Place the kebabs in the air fryer baskets.
4. Return the air fryer basket 1 to Zone 1, and basket 2 to Zone 2 of the Ninja Foodi 2-Basket Air Fryer.
5. Choose the "Air Fry" mode for Zone 1 at 375 degrees F and 18 minutes of cooking time.
6. Select the "MATCH COOK" option to copy the settings for Zone 2.
7. Initiate cooking by pressing the START/PAUSE BUTTON.
8. Flip the kebabs once cooked halfway through.
9. Serve warm.

Mozzarella Stuffed Beef And Pork Meatballs

Servings: 4 To 6
Cooking Time: 12 Minutes

Ingredients:

- 1 tablespoon olive oil
- 1 small onion, finely chopped
- 1 to 2 cloves garlic, minced
- 340 g beef mince
- 340 g pork mince
- 180 ml bread crumbs
- 60 ml grated Parmesan cheese
- 60 ml finely chopped fresh parsley
- ½ teaspoon dried oregano
- 1½ teaspoons salt
- Freshly ground black pepper, to taste
- 2 eggs, lightly beaten
- 140 g low-moisture Mozzarella or other melting cheese, cut into 1-inch cubes

Directions:

1. Preheat a skillet over medium-high heat. Add the oil and cook the onion and garlic until tender, but not browned. 2. Transfer the onion and garlic to a large bowl and add the beef, pork, bread crumbs, Parmesan cheese, parsley, oregano, salt, pepper and eggs. Mix well until all the ingredients are combined. Divide the mixture into 12 evenly sized balls. Make one meatball at a time, by pressing a hole in the meatball mixture with the finger and pushing a piece of Mozzarella cheese into the hole. Mold the meat back into a ball, enclosing the cheese. 3. Preheat the air fryer to 192ºC. 4. Transfer meatballs to the two air fryer drawers and air fry for 12 minutes, shaking the drawers and turning the meatballs twice during the cooking process. Serve warm.

Italian-style Meatballs With Garlicky Roasted Broccoli

Servings: 4
Cooking Time: 15 Minutes

Ingredients:
- FOR THE MEATBALLS
- 1 large egg
- ¼ cup Italian-style bread crumbs
- 1 pound ground beef (85 percent lean)
- ¼ cup grated Parmesan cheese
- ¼ teaspoon kosher salt
- Nonstick cooking spray
- 2 cups marinara sauce
- FOR THE ROASTED BROCCOLI
- 4 cups broccoli florets
- 1 tablespoon olive oil
- ¼ teaspoon kosher salt
- ¼ teaspoon freshly ground pepper
- ¼ teaspoon red pepper flakes
- 1 tablespoon minced garlic

Directions:
1. To prep the meatballs: In a large bowl, beat the egg. Mix in the bread crumbs and let sit for 5 minutes.
2. Add the beef, Parmesan, and salt and mix until just combined. Form the meatball mixture into 8 meatballs, about 1 inch in diameter. Mist with cooking spray.
3. To prep the broccoli: In a large bowl, combine the broccoli, olive oil, salt, black pepper, and red pepper flakes. Toss to coat the broccoli evenly.
4. To cook the meatballs and broccoli: Install a crisper plate in the Zone 1 basket. Place the meatballs in the basket and insert the basket in the unit. Place the broccoli in the Zone 2 basket, sprinkle the garlic over the broccoli, and insert the basket in the unit.
5. Select Zone 1, select AIR FRY, set the temperature to 400°F, and set the time to 12 minutes.
6. Select Zone 2, select ROAST, set the temperature to 390°F, and set the time to 15 minutes. Select SMART FINISH.
7. Press START/PAUSE to begin cooking.
8. When the Zone 1 timer reads 5 minutes, press START/PAUSE. Remove the basket and pour the marinara sauce over the meatballs. Reinsert the basket and press START/PAUSE to resume cooking.
9. When cooking is complete, the meatballs should be cooked through and the broccoli will have begun to brown on the edges.

Nutrition:
- (Per serving) Calories: 493; Total fat: 33g; Saturated fat: 9g; Carbohydrates: 24g; Fiber: 3g; Protein: 31g; Sodium: 926mg

Italian Sausage And Cheese Meatballs

Servings: 4
Cooking Time: 20 Minutes

Ingredients:
- 230 g sausage meat with Italian seasoning added to taste
- 230 g 85% lean beef mince
- 120 ml shredded sharp Cheddar cheese
- ½ teaspoon onion granules
- ½ teaspoon garlic powder
- ½ teaspoon black pepper

Directions:
1. In a large bowl, gently mix the sausage meat, beef mince, cheese, onion granules, garlic powder, and pepper until well combined.
2. Form the mixture into 16 meatballs. Place the meatballs in a single layer in the two air fryer drawers. Set the air fryer to 176°C for 20 minutes, turning the meatballs halfway through the cooking time. Use a meat thermometer to ensure the meatballs have reached an internal temperature of 72°C.

Taco Seasoned Steak

Servings: 6
Cooking Time: 30 Minutes

Ingredients:
- 1 (1-pound) flank steaks
- 1½ tablespoons taco seasoning rub

Directions:
1. Grease each basket of "Zone 1" and "Zone 2" of Ninja Foodi 2-Basket Air Fryer.
2. Press "Zone 1" and "Zone 2" and then rotate the knob for each zone to select "Bake".
3. Set the temperature to 420 degrees F/ 215 degrees C for both zones and then set the time for 5 minutes to preheat.
4. Rub the steaks with taco seasoning evenly.
5. After preheating, arrange the steak into the basket of each zone.
6. Slide each basket into Air Fryer and set the time for 30 minutes.
7. After cooking time is completed, remove the steaks from Air Fryer and place onto a cutting board for about 10-15 minutes before slicing.
8. With a sharp knife, cut each steak into desired size slices and serve.

Turkey And Beef Meatballs

Servings: 6
Cooking Time: 24 Minutes.

Ingredients:

- 1 medium shallot, minced
- 2 tablespoons olive oil
- 3 garlic cloves, minced
- ¼ cup panko crumbs
- 2 tablespoons whole milk
- ⅔ lb. lean ground beef
- ⅓ lb. bulk turkey sausage
- 1 large egg, lightly beaten
- ¼ cup parsley, chopped
- 1 tablespoon fresh thyme, chopped
- 1 tablespoon fresh rosemary, chopped
- 1 tablespoon Dijon mustard
- ½ teaspoon salt

Directions:

1. Preheat your oven to 400 degrees F. Place a medium non-stick pan over medium-high heat.
2. Add oil and shallot, then sauté for 2 minutes.
3. Toss in the garlic and cook for 1 minute.
4. Remove this pan from the heat.
5. Whisk panko with milk in a large bowl and leave it for 5 minutes.
6. Add cooked shallot mixture and mix well.
7. Stir in egg, parsley, turkey sausage, beef, thyme, rosemary, salt, and mustard.
8. Mix well, then divide the mixture into 1 ½-inch balls.
9. Divide these balls into the two crisper plates and spray them with cooking oil.
10. Return the crisper plates to the Ninja Foodi Dual Zone Air Fryer.
11. Choose the Air Fry mode for Zone 1 and set the temperature to 400 degrees F and the time to 21 minutes.
12. Select the "MATCH" button to copy the settings for Zone 2.
13. Initiate cooking by pressing the START/STOP button.
14. Serve warm.

Nutrition:

- (Per serving) Calories 551 | Fat 31g | Sodium 1329mg | Carbs 1.5g | Fiber 0.8g | Sugar 0.4g | Protein 64g

Short Ribs & Root Vegetables

Servings: 2
Cooking Time: 45
Ingredients:

- 1 pound of beef short ribs, bone-in and trimmed
- Salt and black pepper, to taste
- 2 tablespoons canola oil, divided
- 1/4 cup red wine
- 3 tablespoons brown sugar
- 2 cloves garlic, peeled, minced
- 4 carrots, peeled, cut into 1-inch pieces
- 2 parsnips, peeled, cut into 1-inch pieces
- ½ cup pearl onions

Directions:
1. Season the ribs with salt and black pepper and rub a little amount of canola oil on both sides.
2. Place it in zone 1 basket of the air fryer.
3. Next, take a bowl and add pearl onions, parsnip, carrots, garlic, brown sugar, red wine, salt, and black pepper.
4. Add the vegetable mixture to the zone 2 basket.
5. Set the zone 1 basket time to 12 minutes at 375 degrees F at AIR FRY mode.
6. Set the zone 2 basket at AIR FRY mode at 390 degrees F for 18 minutes.
7. Hit start so the cooking cycle being.
8. Once the cooking complete, take out the ingredient and serve short ribs with the mixed vegetables and liquid collect at the bottom of zone 2 basket
9. Enjoy it hot.

Nutrition:
- (Per serving) Calories1262 | Fat 98.6g| Sodium 595mg | Carbs 57g | Fiber 10.1g| Sugar 28.2g | Protein 35.8g

Fish And Seafood Recipes

Lemony Prawns And Courgette

Servings: 4
Cooking Time: 7 To 8 Minutes
Ingredients:

- 570 g extra-large raw prawns, peeled and deveined
- 2 medium courgettes (about 230 g each), halved lengthwise and cut into ½-inch-thick slices
- 1½ tablespoons olive oil
- ½ teaspoon garlic salt
- 1½ teaspoons dried oregano
- ⅛ teaspoon crushed red pepper flakes (optional)
- Juice of ½ lemon
- 1 tablespoon chopped fresh mint
- 1 tablespoon chopped fresh dill

Directions:
1. Preheat the air fryer to 176ºC.
2. In a large bowl, combine the prawns, courgette, oil, garlic salt, oregano, and pepper flakes and toss to coat.
3. Arrange a single layer of the prawns and courgette in the two air fryer drawers. Air fry for 7 to 8 minutes, shaking the drawer halfway, until the courgette is golden and the prawns are cooked through.
4. Transfer to a serving dish and tent with foil while you air fry the remaining prawns and courgette.
5. Top with the lemon juice, mint, and dill and serve.

Salmon Patties

Servings: 8
Cooking Time: 18 Minutes

Ingredients:

- 1 lb. fresh Atlantic salmon side
- ¼ cup avocado, mashed
- ¼ cup cilantro, diced
- 1 ½ teaspoons yellow curry powder
- ½ teaspoons sea salt
- ¼ cup, 4 teaspoons tapioca starch
- 2 brown eggs
- ½ cup coconut flakes
- Coconut oil, melted, for brushing
- For the greens:
- 2 teaspoons organic coconut oil, melted
- 6 cups arugula & spinach mix, tightly packed
- Pinch of sea salt

Directions:

1. Remove the fish skin and dice the flesh.
2. Place in a large bowl. Add cilantro, avocado, salt, and curry powder mix gently.
3. Add tapioca starch and mix well again.
4. Make 8 salmon patties out of this mixture, about a half-inch thick.
5. Place them on a baking sheet lined with wax paper and freeze them for 20 minutes
6. Place ¼ cup tapioca starch and coconut flakes on a flat plate.
7. Dip the patties in the whisked egg, then coat the frozen patties in the starch and flakes.
8. Place half of the patties in each of the crisper plate and spray them with cooking oil
9. Return the crisper plate to the Ninja Foodi Dual Zone Air Fryer.
10. Choose the Air Fry mode for Zone 1 and set the temperature to 390 degrees F and the time to 17 minutes
11. Select the "MATCH" button to copy the settings for Zone 2.
12. Initiate cooking by pressing the START/STOP button.
13. Flip the patties once cooked halfway through, then resume cooking.
14. Sauté arugula with spinach in coconut oil in a pan for 30 seconds.
15. Serve the patties with sautéed greens mixture

Chilean Sea Bass With Olive Relish And Snapper With Tomato

Servings: 4
Cooking Time: 15 Minutes

Ingredients:
- Chilean Sea Bass with Olive Relish:
- Olive oil spray
- 2 (170 g) Chilean sea bass fillets or other firm-fleshed white fish
- 3 tablespoons extra-virgin olive oil
- ½ teaspoon ground cumin
- ½ teaspoon kosher or coarse sea salt
- ½ teaspoon black pepper
- 60 g pitted green olives, diced
- 10 g finely diced onion
- 1 teaspoon chopped capers
- Snapper with Tomato:
- 2 snapper fillets
- 1 shallot, peeled and sliced
- 2 garlic cloves, halved
- 1 bell pepper, sliced
- 1 small-sized serrano pepper, sliced
- 1 tomato, sliced
- 1 tablespoon olive oil
- ¼ teaspoon freshly ground black pepper
- ½ teaspoon paprika
- Sea salt, to taste
- 2 bay leaves

Directions:
1. Make the Chilean Sea Bass with Olive Relish :
2. Spray the zone 1 air fryer drawer with the olive oil spray. Drizzle the fillets with the olive oil and sprinkle with the cumin, salt, and pepper. Place the fish in the zone 1 air fryer drawer. Set the air fryer to 164°C for 10 minutes, or until the fish flakes easily with a fork.
3. Meanwhile, in a small bowl, stir together the olives, onion, and capers.
4. Serve the fish topped with the relish.
5. Make the Snapper with Tomato :
6. Place two baking paper sheets on a working surface. Place the fish in the center of one side of the baking paper.
7. Top with the shallot, garlic, peppers, and tomato. Drizzle olive oil over the fish and vegetables. Season with black pepper, paprika, and salt. Add the bay leaves.
8. Fold over the other half of the baking paper. Now, fold the paper around the edges tightly and create a half moon shape, sealing the fish inside.
9. Cook in the zone 2 air fryer drawer at 200°C for 15 minutes. Serve warm.

Marinated Ginger Garlic Salmon

Servings: 2
Cooking Time: 10 Minutes
Ingredients:
- 2 salmon fillets, skinless & boneless
- 1 1/2 tbsp mirin
- 1 1/2 tbsp soy sauce
- 1 tbsp olive oil
- 2 tbsp green onion, minced
- 1 tbsp ginger, grated
- 1 tsp garlic, minced

Directions:
1. Add mirin, soy sauce, oil, green onion, ginger, and garlic into the zip-lock bag and mix well.
2. Add fish fillets into the bag, seal the bag, and place in the refrigerator for 30 minutes.
3. Preheat the air fryer to 360 F.
4. Spray air fryer basket with cooking spray.
5. Place marinated salmon fillets into the air fryer basket and cook for 10 minutes.
6. Serve and enjoy.

Blackened Red Snapper

Servings: 4
Cooking Time: 8 To 10 Minutes
Ingredients:
- 1½ teaspoons black pepper
- ¼ teaspoon thyme
- ¼ teaspoon garlic powder
- ⅛ teaspoon cayenne pepper
- 1 teaspoon olive oil
- 4 red snapper fillet portions, skin on, 110 g each
- 4 thin slices lemon
- Cooking spray

Directions:
1. Mix the spices and oil together to make a paste. Rub into both sides of the fish.
2. Spray the two air fryer drawers with nonstick cooking spray and lay snapper steaks in drawers, skin-side down.
3. Place a lemon slice on each piece of fish.
4. Roast at 200°C for 8 to 10 minutes. The fish will not flake when done, but it should be white through the center.

Flavorful Salmon With Green Beans

Servings: 4
Cooking Time: 10 Minutes
Ingredients:
- 4 ounces green beans
- 1 tablespoon canola oil
- 4 (6-ounce) salmon fillets
- 1/3 cup prepared sesame-ginger sauce
- Kosher salt, to taste
- Black pepper, to taste

Directions:
1. Toss the green beans with a teaspoon each of salt and pepper in a large bowl.
2. Place a crisper plate in each drawer. Place the green beans in the zone 1 drawer and insert it into the unit. Place the salmon into the zone 2 drawer and place it into the unit.
3. Select zone 1, then AIR FRY, and set the temperature to 390 degrees F/ 200 degrees C with a 10-minute timer.
4. Select zone 2, then AIR FRY, and set the temperature to 390 degrees F/ 200 degrees C with a 15-minute timer. Select SYNC. To begin cooking, press the START/STOP button.
5. Press START/STOP to pause the unit when the zone 2 timer reaches 9 minutes. Remove the salmon from the drawer and toss it in the sesame-ginger sauce. To resume cooking, replace the drawer in the device and press START/STOP.
6. When cooking is complete, serve the salmon and green beans immediately.

Nutrition:
- (Per serving) Calories 305 | Fat 16g | Sodium 535mg | Carbs 8.7g | Fiber 1g | Sugar 6.4g | Protein 34.9g

Seasoned Tuna Steaks

Servings: 4
Cooking Time: 9 Minutes
Ingredients:
- 1 teaspoon garlic powder
- ½ teaspoon salt
- ¼ teaspoon dried thyme
- ¼ teaspoon dried oregano
- 4 tuna steaks
- 2 tablespoons olive oil
- 1 lemon, quartered

Directions:
1. Preheat the air fryer to 190°C.
2. In a small bowl, whisk together the garlic powder, salt, thyme, and oregano.
3. Coat the tuna steaks with olive oil. Season both sides of each steak with the seasoning blend. Place the steaks in a single layer in the two air fryer baskets.
4. Roast for 5 minutes, then flip and roast for an additional 3 to 4 minutes.

Salmon With Broccoli And Cheese

Servings: 2
Cooking Time: 18
Ingredients:

- 2 cups of broccoli
- ½ cup of butter, melted
- Salt and pepper, to taste
- Oil spray, for greasing
- 1 cup of grated cheddar cheese
- 1 pound of salmon, fillets

Directions:
1. Take a bowl and add broccoli to it.
2. Add salt and black pepper and spray it with oil.
3. Put the broccoli in the air fryer zone 1 backset.
4. Now rub the salmon fillets with salt, black pepper, and butter.
5. Put it into zone 2 baskets.
6. Set zone 1 to air fry mode for 5 minters at 400 degrees F.
7. Set zone 2 to air fry mode for 18 minutes at 390 degrees F.
8. Hit start to start the cooking.
9. Once done, serve and by placing it on serving plates.
10. Put the grated cheese on top of the salmon and serve.

Nutrition:
- (Per serving) Calories 966 | Fat 79.1 g | Sodium 808 mg | Carbs 6.8 g | Fiber 2.4g | Sugar 1.9g | Protein 61.2 g

Codfish With Herb Vinaigrette

Servings: 2
Cooking Time: 16
Ingredients:

- Vinaigrette Ingredients:
- 1/2 cup parsley leaves
- 1 cup basil leaves
- ½ cup mint leaves
- 2 tablespoons thyme leaves
- 1/4 teaspoon red pepper flakes
- 2 cloves of garlic
- 4 tablespoons of red wine vinegar
- ¼ cup of olive oil
- Salt, to taste
- Other Ingredients:
- 1.5 pounds fish fillets, cod fish
- 2 tablespoons olive oil
- Salt and black pepper, to taste
- 1 teaspoon of paprika
- 1teasbpoon of Italian seasoning

Directions:
1. Blend the entire vinaigrette ingredient in a high-speed blender and pulse into a smooth paste.
2. Set aside for drizzling overcooked fish.
3. Rub the fillets with salt, black pepper, paprika, Italian seasoning, and olive oil.
4. Divide it between two baskets of the air fryer.
5. Set the zone 1 to 16 minutes at 390 degrees F, at AIR FRY mode.
6. Press the MATCH button for the second basket.
7. Once done, serve the fillets with the drizzle of blended vinaigrette

Nutrition:
- (Per serving) Calories 1219| Fat 81.8g| Sodium 1906mg | Carbs64.4 g | Fiber5.5 g | Sugar 0.4g | Protein 52.1g

Orange-mustard Glazed Salmon And Cucumber And Salmon Salad

Servings: 4
Cooking Time: 10 Minutes

Ingredients:

- Orange-Mustard Glazed Salmon:
- 1 tablespoon orange marmalade
- ¼ teaspoon grated orange zest plus 1 tablespoon juice
- 2 teaspoons whole-grain mustard
- 2 (230 g) skin-on salmon fillets, 1½ inches thick
- Salt and pepper, to taste
- Vegetable oil spray
- Cucumber and Salmon Salad:
- 455 g salmon fillet
- 1½ tablespoons olive oil, divided
- 1 tablespoon sherry vinegar
- 1 tablespoon capers, rinsed and drained
- 1 seedless cucumber, thinly sliced
- ¼ white onion, thinly sliced
- 2 tablespoons chopped fresh parsley
- Salt and freshly ground black pepper, to taste

Directions:

1. Make the Orange-Mustard Glazed Salmon :
2. Preheat the air fryer to 205°C.
3. Make foil sling for air fryer basket by folding 1 long sheet of aluminum foil so it is 4 inches wide. Lay sheet of foil widthwise across zone 1 basket, pressing foil into and up sides of basket. Fold excess foil as needed so that edges of foil are flush with top of basket. Lightly spray foil and basket with vegetable oil spray.
4. Combine marmalade, orange zest and juice, and mustard in bowl. Pat salmon dry with paper towels and season with salt and pepper. Brush tops and sides of fillets evenly with glaze. Arrange fillets skin side down on sling in prepared zone 1 basket, spaced evenly apart. Air fry salmon until center is still translucent when checked with the tip of a paring knife and registers 50°C , 10 to 14 minutes, using sling to rotate fillets halfway through cooking.
5. Using the sling, carefully remove salmon from air fryer. Slide fish spatula along underside of fillets and transfer to individual serving plates, leaving skin behind. Serve.
6. Make the Cucumber and Salmon Salad :
7. Preheat the air fryer to 205°C.
8. Lightly coat the salmon with ½ tablespoon of the olive oil. Place skin-side down in the zone 2 air fryer basket and air fry for 8 to 10 minutes until the fish is opaque and flakes easily with a fork. Transfer the salmon to a plate and let cool to room temperature. Remove the skin and carefully flake the fish into bite-size chunks.
9. In a small bowl, whisk the remaining 1 tablespoon olive oil and the vinegar until thoroughly combined. Add the flaked fish, capers, cucumber, onion, and parsley. Season to taste with salt and freshly ground black pepper. Toss gently to coat. Serve immediately or cover and refrigerate for up to 4 hours.

Lemon Pepper Salmon With Asparagus

Servings: 2
Cooking Time: 18
Ingredients:
- 1 cup of green asparagus
- 2 tablespoons of butter
- 2 fillets of salmon, 8 ounces each
- Salt and black pepper, to taste
- 1 teaspoon of lemon juice
- ½ teaspoon of lemon zest
- oil spray, for greasing

Directions:
1. Rinse and trim the asparagus.
2. Rinse and pat dry the salmon fillets.
3. Take a bowl and mix lemon juice, lemon zest, salt, and black pepper.
4. Brush the fish fillet with the rub and place it in the zone 1 basket.
5. Place asparagus in zone 2 basket.
6. Spray the asparagus with oil spray.
7. Set zone 1 to AIRFRY mode for 18 minutes at 390 degrees F.
8. Set the zone 2 to 5 minutes at 390 degrees F, at air fry mode.
9. Hit the smart finish button to finish at the same time.
10. Once done, serve and enjoy.

Nutrition:
- (Per serving) Calories 482| Fat 28g| Sodium209 mg | Carbs 2.8g | Fiber1.5 g | Sugar1.4 g | Protein 56.3g

Coconut Cream Mackerel

Servings: 4
Cooking Time: 6 Minutes
Ingredients:
- 900 g mackerel fillet
- 240 ml coconut cream
- 1 teaspoon ground coriander
- 1 teaspoon cumin seeds
- 1 garlic clove, peeled, chopped

Directions:
1. Chop the mackerel roughly and sprinkle it with coconut cream, ground coriander, cumin seeds, and garlic.
2. Then put the fish in the two air fryer drawers and cook at 204°C for 6 minutes.

Salmon Fritters With Courgette & Cajun And Lemon Pepper Cod

Servings: 6
Cooking Time: 12 Minutes

Ingredients:
- Salmon Fritters with Courgette:
- 2 tablespoons almond flour
- 1 courgette, grated
- 1 egg, beaten
- 170 g salmon fillet, diced
- 1 teaspoon avocado oil
- ½ teaspoon ground black pepper
- Cajun and Lemon Pepper Cod:
- 1 tablespoon Cajun seasoning
- 1 teaspoon salt
- ½ teaspoon lemon pepper
- ½ teaspoon freshly ground black pepper
- 2 cod fillets, 230 g each, cut to fit into the air fryer basket
- Cooking spray
- 2 tablespoons unsalted butter, melted
- 1 lemon, cut into 4 wedges

Directions:
1. Make the Salmon Fritters with Courgette :
2. Mix almond flour with courgette, egg, salmon, and ground black pepper.
3. Then make the fritters from the salmon mixture.
4. Sprinkle the zone 1 air fryer basket with avocado oil and put the fritters inside.
5. Cook the fritters at 190°C for 6 minutes per side.
6. Make the Cajun and Lemon Pepper Cod :
7. Preheat the air fryer to 180°C. Spritz the zone 2 air fryer basket with cooking spray.
8. Thoroughly combine the Cajun seasoning, salt, lemon pepper, and black pepper in a small bowl. Rub this mixture all over the cod fillets until completely coated.
9. Put the fillets in the air fryer basket and brush the melted butter over both sides of each fillet.
10. Bake in the preheated air fryer for 12 minutes, flipping the fillets halfway through, or until the fish flakes easily with a fork.
11. Remove the fillets from the basket and serve with fresh lemon wedges.

Fish Tacos

Servings: 5
Cooking Time: 30 Minutes

Ingredients:
- 1 pound firm white fish such as cod, haddock, pollock, halibut, or walleye
- ¾ cup gluten-free flour blend
- 3 eggs
- 1 cup gluten-free panko breadcrumbs
- 1 teaspoon garlic powder
- 1 teaspoon onion powder
- 1 teaspoon cumin
- 1 teaspoon lemon pepper
- 1 teaspoon red chili flakes
- 1 teaspoon kosher salt, divided
- 1 teaspoon pepper, divided
- Cooking oil spray
- 1 package corn tortillas
- Toppings such as tomatoes, avocado, cabbage, radishes, jalapenos, salsa, or hot sauce (optional)

Directions:
1. Dry the fish with paper towels. (Make sure to thaw the fish if it's frozen.) Depending on the size of the fillets, cut the fish in half or thirds.
2. On both sides of the fish pieces, liberally season with salt and pepper.
3. Put the flour in a dish.
4. In a separate bowl, crack the eggs and whisk them together until well blended.
5. Put the panko breadcrumbs in another bowl. Add the garlic powder, onion powder, cumin, lemon pepper, and red chili flakes. Add salt and pepper to taste. Stir until everything is well blended.
6. Each piece of fish should be dipped in the flour, then the eggs, and finally in the breadcrumb mixture. Make sure that each piece is completely coated.
7. Put a crisper plate in each drawer. Arrange the fish pieces in a single layer in each drawer. Insert the drawers into the unit.
8. Select zone 1, then AIR FRY, then set the temperature to 360 degrees F/ 180 degrees C with a 20-minute timer. To match zone 2 settings to zone 1, choose MATCH. To begin, select START/STOP.
9. Remove the fish from the drawers after the timer has finished. Place the crispy fish on warmed tortillas.

Nutrition:
- (Per serving) Calories 534 | Fat 18g | Sodium 679mg | Carbs 63g | Fiber 8g | Sugar 3g | Protein 27g

Steamed Cod With Garlic And Swiss Chard

Servings: 4
Cooking Time: 12 Minutes
Ingredients:
- 1 teaspoon salt
- ½ teaspoon dried oregano
- ½ teaspoon dried thyme
- ½ teaspoon garlic powder
- 4 cod fillets
- ½ white onion, thinly sliced
- 135 g Swiss chard, washed, stemmed, and torn into pieces
- 60 ml olive oil
- 1 lemon, quartered

Directions:
1. Preheat the air fryer to 192°C.
2. In a small bowl, whisk together the salt, oregano, thyme, and garlic powder.
3. Tear off four pieces of aluminum foil, with each sheet being large enough to envelop one cod fillet and a quarter of the vegetables.
4. Place a cod fillet in the middle of each sheet of foil, then sprinkle on all sides with the spice mixture.
5. In each foil packet, place a quarter of the onion slices and 30 g Swiss chard, then drizzle 1 tablespoon olive oil and squeeze ¼ lemon over the contents of each foil packet.
6. Fold and seal the sides of the foil packets and then place them into the two air fryer drawers. Steam for 12 minutes.
7. Remove from the drawers, and carefully open each packet to avoid a steam burn.

Italian Baked Cod

Servings: 4
Cooking Time: 12 Minutes
Ingredients:
- 4 cod fillets, 170 g each
- 2 tablespoons salted butter, melted
- 1 teaspoon Italian seasoning
- ¼ teaspoon salt
- 120 ml tomato-based pasta sauce

Directions:
1. Place cod into an ungreased round nonstick baking dish. Pour butter over cod and sprinkle with Italian seasoning and salt. Top with pasta sauce.
2. Place dish into the two air fryer drawers. Adjust the temperature to 176°C and bake for 12 minutes. Fillets will be lightly browned, easily flake, and have an internal temperature of at least 64°C when done. Serve warm.

Scallops And Spinach With Cream Sauce And Confetti Salmon Burgers

Servings: 6
Cooking Time: 12 Minutes

Ingredients:
- Scallops and Spinach with Cream Sauce:
- Vegetable oil spray
- 280 g frozen spinach, thawed and drained
- 8 jumbo sea scallops
- Kosher or coarse sea salt, and black pepper, to taste
- 180 ml heavy cream
- 1 tablespoon tomato paste
- 1 tablespoon chopped fresh basil
- 1 teaspoon minced garlic
- Confetti Salmon Burgers:
- 400 g cooked fresh or canned salmon, flaked with a fork
- 40 g minced spring onions, white and light green parts only
- 40 g minced red bell pepper
- 40 g minced celery
- 2 small lemons
- 1 teaspoon crab boil seasoning such as Old Bay
- ½ teaspoon kosher or coarse sea salt
- ½ teaspoon black pepper
- 1 egg, beaten
- 30 g fresh bread crumbs
- Vegetable oil, for spraying

Directions:
1. Make the Scallops and Spinach with Cream Sauce :
2. Spray a baking pan with vegetable oil spray. Spread the thawed spinach in an even layer in the bottom of the pan.
3. Spray both sides of the scallops with vegetable oil spray. Season lightly with salt and pepper. Arrange the scallops on top of the spinach.
4. In a small bowl, whisk together the cream, tomato paste, basil, garlic, ½ teaspoon salt, and ½ teaspoon pepper. Pour the sauce over the scallops and spinach.
5. Place the pan in the zone 1 air fryer drawer. Set the temperature to 176°C for 10 minutes. Use a meat thermometer to ensure the scallops have an internal temperature of 56°C.
6. Make the Confetti Salmon Burgers :
7. In a large bowl, combine the salmon, vegetables, the zest and juice of 1 of the lemons, crab boil seasoning, salt, and pepper. Add the egg and bread crumbs and stir to combine. Form the mixture into 4 patties weighing approximately 140 g each. Chill until firm, about 15 minutes.
8. Preheat the 2 air fryer drawer to 204°C.
9. Spray the salmon patties with oil on all sides and spray the zone 2 air fryer drawer to prevent sticking. Air fry for 12 minutes, flipping halfway through, until the burgers are browned and cooked through. Cut the remaining lemon into 4 wedges and serve with the burgers.

Prawns Curry

Servings: 4
Cooking Time: 10 Minutes
Ingredients:

- 180 ml unsweetened full-fat coconut milk
- 10 g finely chopped yellow onion
- 2 teaspoons garam masala
- 1 tablespoon minced fresh ginger
- 1 tablespoon minced garlic
- 1 teaspoon ground turmeric
- 1 teaspoon salt
- ¼ to ½ teaspoon cayenne pepper
- 455 g raw prawns (21 to 25 count), peeled and deveined
- 2 teaspoons chopped fresh coriander

Directions:
1. In a large bowl, stir together the coconut milk, onion, garam masala, ginger, garlic, turmeric, salt and cayenne, until well blended.
2. Add the prawns and toss until coated with sauce on all sides. Marinate at room temperature for 30 minutes.
3. Transfer the prawns and marinade to a baking pan. Place the pan in the zone 1 air fryer drawer. Set the temperature to 192°C for 10 minutes, stirring halfway through the cooking time.
4. Transfer the prawns to a serving bowl or platter. Sprinkle with the cilantro and serve.

Honey Pecan Shrimp

Servings: 4
Cooking Time: 10 Minutes
Ingredients:

- ¼ cup cornstarch
- ¾ teaspoon salt
- ¼ teaspoon black pepper
- 2 egg whites
- ⅔ cup pecans, chopped
- 455g shrimp, peeled, and deveined
- ¼ cup honey
- 2 tablespoons mayonnaise

Directions:
1. Mix cornstarch with ½ teaspoon black pepper, and ½ teaspoon salt in a bowl.
2. Mix pecans and ¼ teaspoon salt in another bowl.
3. Beat egg whites in another bowl.
4. Dredge the shrimp through the cornstarch mixture then dip in the egg whites.
5. Coat the shrimp with pecans mixture.
6. Divide the coated shrimp in the air fryer baskets.
7. Return the air fryer basket 1 to Zone 1, and basket 2 to Zone 2 of the Ninja Foodi 2-Basket Air Fryer.
8. Choose the "Air Fry" mode for Zone 1 at 330 degrees F and 10 minutes of cooking time.
9. Select the "MATCH COOK" option to copy the settings for Zone 2.
10. Initiate cooking by pressing the START/PAUSE BUTTON.
11. Flip the shrimps once cooked halfway through.
12. Serve.

Nutrition:
- (Per serving) Calories 155 | Fat 4.2g | Sodium 963mg | Carbs 21.5g | Fiber 0.8g | Sugar 5.7g | Protein 8.1g

Honey Teriyaki Salmon

Servings: 3
Cooking Time: 12 Minutes
Ingredients:
- 8 tablespoon teriyaki sauce
- 3 tablespoons honey
- 2 cubes frozen garlic
- 2 tablespoons olive oil
- 3 pieces wild salmon

Directions:
1. Mix teriyaki sauce, honey, garlic and oil in a large bowl.
2. Add salmon to this sauce and mix well to coat.
3. Cover and refrigerate the salmon for 20 minutes.
4. Place the salmon pieces in one air fryer basket.
5. Return the air fryer basket 1 to Zone 1 of the Ninja Foodi 2-Basket Air Fryer.
6. Choose the "Air Fry" mode for Zone 1 and set the temperature to 350 degrees F and 12 minutes of cooking time.
7. Initiate cooking by pressing the START/PAUSE BUTTON.
8. Flip the pieces once cooked halfway through.
9. Serve warm.

Nutrition:
- (Per serving) Calories 260 | Fat 16g |Sodium 585mg | Carbs 3.1g | Fiber 1.3g | Sugar 0.2g | Protein 25.5g

Vegetables And Sides Recipes

Mushroom Roll-ups

Servings: 10
Cooking Time: 10 Minutes
Ingredients:
- 2 tablespoons extra virgin olive oil
- 8 ounces large portobello mushrooms (gills discarded), finely chopped
- 1 teaspoon dried oregano
- 1 teaspoon dried thyme
- ½ teaspoon crushed red pepper flakes
- ¼ teaspoon salt
- 8 ounces cream cheese, softened
- 4 ounces whole-milk ricotta cheese
- 10 flour tortillas (8-inch)
- Cooking spray
- Chutney, for serving (optional)

Directions:
1. Heat the oil in a pan over medium heat. Add the mushrooms and cook for 4 minutes. Sauté until the mushrooms are browned, about 4-6 minutes, with the oregano, thyme, pepper flakes, and salt. Cool.
2. Combine the cheeses in a mixing bowl| fold in the mushrooms until thoroughly combined.
3. On the bottom center of each tortilla, spread 3 tablespoons of the mushroom mixture. Tightly roll up each tortilla and secure with toothpicks.
4. Place a crisper plate in each drawer. Put the roll-ups in a single layer in each. Insert the drawers into the unit.
5. Select zone 1, then AIR FRY, then set the temperature to 400 degrees F/ 200 degrees C with a 10-minute timer. To match zone 2 settings to zone 1, choose MATCH. To begin, select START/STOP.
6. Remove the roll-ups from the drawers after the timer has finished. When they have cooled enough to handle, discard the toothpicks.
7. Serve and enjoy!

Air-fried Tofu Cutlets With Cacio E Pepe Brussels Sprouts

Servings: 4
Cooking Time: 25 Minutes

Ingredients:
- FOR THE TOFU CUTLETS
- 1 (14-ounce) package extra-firm tofu, drained
- 1 cup panko bread crumbs
- ¼ cup grated pecorino romano or Parmesan cheese
- 1 teaspoon garlic powder
- 1 teaspoon onion powder
- ¼ teaspoon kosher salt
- 1 tablespoon vegetable oil
- 4 lemon wedges, for serving
- FOR THE BRUSSELS SPROUTS
- 1 pound Brussels sprouts, trimmed
- 1 tablespoon vegetable oil
- 2 tablespoons grated pecorino romano or Parmesan cheese
- ½ teaspoon freshly ground black pepper, plus more to taste
- ¼ teaspoon kosher salt

Directions:
1. To prep the tofu: Cut the tofu horizontally into 4 slabs.
2. In a shallow bowl, mix together the panko, cheese, garlic powder, onion powder, and salt. Press both sides of each tofu slab into the panko mixture. Drizzle both sides with the oil.
3. To prep the Brussels sprouts: Cut the Brussels sprouts in half through the root end.
4. In a large bowl, combine the Brussels sprouts and olive oil. Mix to coat.
5. To cook the tofu cutlets and Brussels sprouts: Install a crisper plate in each of the two baskets. Place the tofu cutlets in a single layer in the Zone 1 basket and insert the basket in the unit. Place the Brussels sprouts in the Zone 2 basket and insert the basket in the unit.
6. Select Zone 1, select AIR FRY, set the temperature to 400°F, and set the timer to 20 minutes.
7. Select Zone 2, select ROAST, set the temperature to 400°F, and set the timer to 25 minutes. Select SMART FINISH.
8. Press START/PAUSE to begin cooking.
9. When both timers read 5 minutes, press START/PAUSE. Remove the Zone 1 basket and use a pair of silicone-tipped tongs to flip the tofu cutlets, then reinsert the basket in the unit. Remove the Zone 2 basket and sprinkle the cheese and black pepper over the Brussels sprouts. Reinsert the basket and press START/PAUSE to resume cooking.
10. When cooking is complete, the tofu should be crisp and the Brussels sprouts tender and beginning to brown.
11. Squeeze the lemon wedges over the tofu cutlets. Stir the Brussels sprouts, then season with the salt and additional black pepper to taste.

Nutrition:
- (Per serving) Calories: 319; Total fat: 15g; Saturated fat: 3.5g; Carbohydrates: 27g; Fiber: 6g; Protein: 20g; Sodium: 402mg

Buffalo Seitan With Crispy Zucchini Noodles

Servings: 4
Cooking Time: 12 Minutes

Ingredients:
- FOR THE BUFFALO SEITAN
- 1 (8-ounce) package precooked seitan strips
- 1 teaspoon garlic powder, divided
- ½ teaspoon onion powder
- ¼ teaspoon smoked paprika
- ¼ cup Louisiana-style hot sauce
- 2 tablespoons vegetable oil
- 1 tablespoon tomato paste
- ¼ teaspoon freshly ground black pepper
- FOR THE ZUCCHINI NOODLES
- 3 large egg whites
- 1¼ cups all-purpose flour
- 1 teaspoon kosher salt, divided
- 12 ounces seltzer water or club soda
- 5 ounces zucchini noodles
- Nonstick cooking spray

Directions:
1. To prep the Buffalo seitan: Season the seitan strips with ½ teaspoon of garlic powder, the onion powder, and smoked paprika.
2. In a large bowl, whisk together the hot sauce, oil, tomato paste, remaining ½ teaspoon of garlic powder, and the black pepper. Set the bowl of Buffalo sauce aside.
3. To prep the zucchini noodles: In a medium bowl, use a handheld mixer to beat the egg whites until stiff peaks form.
4. In a large bowl, combine the flour and ½ teaspoon of salt. Mix in the seltzer to form a thin batter. Fold in the beaten egg whites.
5. Add the zucchini to the batter and gently mix to coat.
6. To cook the seitan and zucchini noodles: Install a crisper plate in each of the two baskets. Place the seitan in the Zone 1 basket and insert the basket in the unit. Lift the noodles from the batter one at a time, letting the excess drip off, and place them in the Zone 2 basket. Insert the basket in the unit.
7. Select Zone 1, select BAKE, set the temperature to 370°F, and set the timer to 12 minutes.
8. Select Zone 2, select AIR FRY, set the temperature to 400°F, and set the timer to 12 minutes. Select SMART FINISH.
9. Press START/PAUSE to begin cooking.
10. When the Zone 1 timer reads 2 minutes, press START/PAUSE. Remove the basket and transfer the seitan to the bowl of Buffalo sauce. Turn to coat, then return the seitan to the basket. Reinsert the basket and press START/PAUSE to resume cooking.
11. When cooking is complete, the seitan should be warmed through and the zucchini noodles crisp and light golden brown.
12. Sprinkle the zucchini noodles with the remaining ½ teaspoon of salt. If desired, drizzle extra Buffalo sauce over the seitan. Serve hot.

Nutrition:
- (Per serving) Calories: 252; Total fat: 15g; Saturated fat: 1g; Carbohydrates: 22g; Fiber: 1.5g; Protein: 13g; Sodium: 740mg

Quinoa Patties

Servings: 4
Cooking Time: 32 Minutes

Ingredients:
- 1 cup quinoa red
- 1½ cups water
- 1 teaspoon salt
- black pepper, ground
- 1½ cups rolled oats
- 3 eggs beaten
- ¼ cup minced white onion
- ½ cup crumbled feta cheese
- ¼ cup chopped fresh chives
- Salt and black pepper, to taste
- Vegetable or canola oil
- 4 hamburger buns
- 4 arugulas
- 4 slices tomato sliced
- Cucumber yogurt dill sauce
- 1 cup cucumber, diced
- 1 cup Greek yogurt
- 2 teaspoons lemon juice
- ¼ teaspoon salt
- Black pepper, ground
- 1 tablespoon chopped fresh dill
- 1 tablespoon olive oil

Directions:
1. Add quinoa to a saucepan filled with cold water, salt, and black pepper, and place it over medium-high heat.
2. Cook the quinoa to a boil, then reduce the heat, cover, and cook for 20 minutes on a simmer.
3. Fluff and mix the cooked quinoa with a fork and remove it from the heat.
4. Spread the quinoa in a baking stay.
5. Mix eggs, oats, onion, herbs, cheese, salt, and black pepper.
6. Stir in quinoa, then mix well. Make 4 patties out of this quinoa cheese mixture.
7. Divide the patties in the two crisper plates and spray them with cooking oil. 8. Return the crisper plates to the Ninja Foodi Dual Zone Air Fryer.
8. Choose the Air Fry mode for Zone 1 and set the temperature to 390 degrees F/ 200 degrees C and the time to 13 minutes.
9. Select the "MATCH" button to copy the settings for Zone 2.
10. Initiate cooking by pressing the START/STOP button.
11. Flip the patties once cooked halfway through, and resume cooking.
12. Meanwhile, prepare the cucumber yogurt dill sauce by mixing all of its ingredients in a mixing bowl.
13. Place each quinoa patty in a burger bun along with arugula leaves.
14. Serve with yogurt dill sauce.

Balsamic-glazed Tofu With Roasted Butternut Squash

Servings: 4
Cooking Time: 40 Minutes

Ingredients:
- FOR THE BALSAMIC TOFU
- 2 tablespoons balsamic vinegar
- 1 tablespoon maple syrup
- 1 teaspoon soy sauce
- 1 teaspoon Dijon mustard
- 1 (14-ounce) package firm tofu, drained and cut into large cubes
- 1 tablespoon canola oil
- FOR THE BUTTERNUT SQUASH
- 1 small butternut squash
- 1 tablespoon canola oil
- 1 teaspoon light brown sugar
- ¼ teaspoon kosher salt
- ¼ teaspoon freshly ground black pepper

Directions:
1. To prep the balsamic tofu: In a large bowl, whisk together the vinegar, maple syrup, soy sauce, and mustard. Add the tofu and stir to coat. Cover and marinate for at least 20 minutes (or up to overnight in the refrigerator).
2. To prep the butternut squash: Peel the squash and cut in half lengthwise. Remove and discard the seeds. Cut the squash crosswise into ½-inch-thick slices.
3. Brush the squash pieces with the oil, then sprinkle with the brown sugar, salt, and black pepper.
4. To cook the tofu and squash: Install a crisper plate in each of the two baskets. Place the tofu in the Zone 1 basket, drizzle with the oil, and insert the basket in the unit. Place the squash in the Zone 2 basket and insert the basket in the unit.
5. Select Zone 1, select AIR FRY, set the temperature to 400°F, and set the timer to 10 minutes.
6. Select Zone 2, select ROAST, set the temperature to 400°F, and set the timer to 40 minutes. Select SMART FINISH.
7. Press START/PAUSE to begin cooking.
8. When cooking is complete, the tofu will have begun to crisp and brown around the edges and the squash should be tender. Serve hot.

Nutrition:
- (Per serving) Calories: 253; Total fat: 11g; Saturated fat: 1g; Carbohydrates: 30g; Fiber: 4.5g; Protein: 11g; Sodium: 237mg

Bbq Corn

Servings: 4
Cooking Time: 10 Minutes

Ingredients:
- 450g can baby corn, drained & rinsed
- 56g BBQ sauce
- ½ tsp Sriracha sauce

Directions:
1. In a bowl, toss the baby corn with sriracha sauce and BBQ sauce until well coated.
2. Insert a crisper plate in the Ninja Foodi air fryer baskets.
3. Add the baby corn to both baskets.
4. Select zone 1, then select "air fry" mode and set the temperature to 390 degrees F for 10 minutes. Press "match" to match zone 2 settings to zone 1. Press "start/stop" to begin. Stir halfway through.

Nutrition:
- (Per serving) Calories 46 | Fat 0.1g |Sodium 446mg | Carbs 10.2g | Fiber 2.8g | Sugar 5.9g | Protein 0.9g

Garlic-rosemary Brussels Sprouts

Servings: 4
Cooking Time: 15 Minutes

Ingredients:
- 3 tablespoons olive oil
- 2 garlic cloves, minced
- ½ teaspoon salt
- ¼ teaspoon pepper
- 1-pound Brussels sprouts, trimmed and halved
- ½ cup panko breadcrumbs
- 1½ teaspoons minced fresh rosemary

Directions:
1. Place the first 4 ingredients in a small microwave-safe bowl| microwave on high for 30 seconds.
2. Toss the Brussels sprouts in 2 tablespoons of the microwaved mixture.
3. Place a crisper plate in each drawer. Put the sprouts in a single layer in each drawer. Insert the drawers into the units.
4. Select zone 1, then AIR FRY, then set the temperature to 360 degrees F/ 180 degrees C with a 6-minute timer. To match zone 2 settings to zone 1, choose MATCH. To begin, select START/STOP.
5. Remove the sprouts from the drawers after the timer has finished.
6. Toss the breadcrumbs with the rosemary and remaining oil mixture| sprinkle over the sprouts.
7. Continue cooking until the crumbs are browned, and the sprouts are tender . Serve immediately.

Garlic Herbed Baked Potatoes

Servings: 4
Cooking Time: 45 Minutes
Ingredients:

- 4 large baking potatoes
- Salt and black pepper, to taste
- 2 teaspoons avocado oil
- Cheese
- 2 cups sour cream
- 1 teaspoon garlic clove, minced
- 1 teaspoon fresh dill
- 2 teaspoons chopped chives
- Salt and black pepper, to taste
- 2 teaspoons Worcestershire sauce

Directions:
1. Pierce the skin of the potatoes with a fork.
2. Season the potatoes with olive oil, salt, and black pepper.
3. Divide the potatoes into the air fryer baskets.
4. Now press 1 for zone 1 and set it to AIR FRY mode at 350 degrees F/ 175 degrees C, for 45 minutes.
5. Select the MATCH button for zone 2.
6. Meanwhile, take a bowl and mix all the cheese ingredients together.
7. Once the cooking cycle is complete, take out the potatoes and make a slit in-between each one.
8. Add the cheese mixture in the cavity and serve it hot.

Balsamic Vegetables

Servings: 4
Cooking Time: 13 Minutes
Ingredients:

- 125g asparagus, cut woody ends
- 88g mushrooms, halved
- 1 tbsp Dijon mustard
- 3 tbsp soy sauce
- 27g brown sugar
- 57ml balsamic vinegar
- 32g olive oil
- 1 zucchini, sliced
- 1 yellow squash, sliced
- 170g grape tomatoes
- Pepper
- Salt

Directions:
1. In a bowl, mix asparagus, tomatoes, oil, mustard, soy sauce, mushrooms, zucchini, squash, brown sugar, vinegar, pepper, and salt.
2. Cover the bowl and place it in the refrigerator for 45 minutes.
3. Insert a crisper plate in the Ninja Foodi air fryer baskets.
4. Add the vegetable mixture in both baskets.
5. Select zone 1, then select "air fry" mode and set the temperature to 390 degrees F for 12 minutes. Press "match" to match zone 2 settings to zone 1. Press "start/stop" to begin. Stir halfway through.

Nutrition:
- (Per serving) Calories 184 | Fat 13.3g |Sodium 778mg | Carbs 14.7g | Fiber 3.6g | Sugar 9.5g | Protein 5.5g

Fresh Mix Veggies In Air Fryer

Servings: 4
Cooking Time: 12 Minutes

Ingredients:

- 1 cup cauliflower florets
- 1 cup carrots, peeled chopped
- 1 cup broccoli florets
- 2 tablespoons avocado oil
- Salt, to taste
- ½ teaspoon chili powder
- ½ teaspoon garlic powder
- ½ teaspoon herbs de Provence
- 1 cup Parmesan cheese

Directions:

1. Take a bowl, and add all the veggies to it.
2. Toss and then season the veggies with salt, chili powder, garlic powder, and herbs de Provence.
3. Toss it all well and then drizzle avocado oil.
4. Make sure the ingredients are coated well.
5. Distribute the veggies among both baskets of the air fryer.
6. Turn on the START/STOP button and set it to AIR FRY mode at 390 degrees F/ 200 degrees C for 10-12 minutes.
7. For the zone 2 basket setting, press the MATCH button.
8. After 8 minutes of cooking, press the START/STOP button and then take out the baskets and sprinkle Parmesan cheese on top of the veggies.
9. Then let the cooking cycle complete for the next 3-4 minutes.
10. Once done, serve.

Garlic Potato Wedges In Air Fryer

Servings: 2
Cooking Time: 23 Minutes

Ingredients:

- 4 medium potatoes, peeled and cut into wedges
- 4 tablespoons butter
- 1 teaspoon chopped cilantro
- 1 cup plain flour
- 1 teaspoon garlic, minced
- Salt and black pepper, to taste

Directions:

1. Soak the potato wedges in cold water for about 30 minutes.
2. Drain and pat dry with a paper towel.
3. Boil water in a large pot and boil the wedges for 3 minutes and place on a paper towel.
4. In a bowl, mix garlic, melted butter, salt, pepper, and cilantro.
5. Add the flour to a separate bowl along with the salt and black pepper.
6. Add water to the flour so it gets a runny in texture.
7. Coat the potatoes with the flour mixture and divide them into two foil tins. 8. Place the foil tins in each air fryer basket.
8. Set the zone 1 basket to AIR FRY mode at 390 degrees F/ 200 degrees C for 20 minutes.
9. Select the MATCH button for the zone 2 basket. 11. Once done, serve and enjoy.

Pepper Poppers

Servings: 24
Cooking Time: 20 Minutes

Ingredients:

- 8 ounces cream cheese, softened
- ¾ cup shredded cheddar cheese
- ¾ cup shredded Monterey Jack cheese
- 6 bacon strips, cooked and crumbled
- ¼ teaspoon salt
- ¼ teaspoon garlic powder
- ¼ teaspoon chili powder
- ¼ teaspoon smoked paprika
- 1-pound fresh jalapeño peppers, halved lengthwise and deseeded
- ½ cup dry breadcrumbs
- Sour cream, French onion dip, or ranch salad dressing (optional)

Directions:

1. In a large bowl, combine the cheeses, bacon, and seasonings| mix well. Spoon 1½ to 2 tablespoons of the mixture into each pepper half. Roll them in the breadcrumbs.
2. Place a crisper plate in each drawer. Put the prepared peppers in a single layer in each drawer. Insert the drawers into the unit.
3. Select zone 1, then AIR FRY, then set the temperature to 360 degrees F/ 180 degrees C with a 20-minute timer. To match zone 2 settings to zone 1, choose MATCH. To begin, select START/STOP.
4. Remove the peppers from the drawers after the timer has finished.

Zucchini With Stuffing

Servings: 3
Cooking Time: 20

Ingredients:

- 1 cup quinoa, rinsed
- 1 cup black olives
- 6 medium zucchinis, about 2 pounds
- 2 cups cannellini beans, drained
- 1 white onion, chopped
- ¼ cup almonds, chopped
- 4 cloves of garlic, chopped
- 4 tablespoons olive oil
- 1 cup of water
- 2 cups Parmesan cheese, for topping

Directions:

1. First wash the zucchini and cut it lengthwise.
2. Take a skillet and heat oil in it
3. Sauté the onion in olive oil for a few minutes.
4. Then add the quinoa and water and let it cook for 8 minutes with the lid on the top.
5. Transfer the quinoa to a bowl and add all remaining ingredients excluding zucchini and Parmesan cheese.
6. Scoop out the seeds of zucchinis.
7. Fill the cavity of zucchinis with bowl mixture.
8. Top it with a handful of Parmesan cheese.
9. Arrange 4 zucchinis in both air fryer baskets.
10. Select zone1 basket at AIR FRY for 20 minutes and adjusting the temperature to 390 degrees F.
11. Use the Match button to select the same setting for zone 2.
12. Serve and enjoy.

Nutrition:

- (Per serving) Calories 1171| Fat 48.6g| Sodium 1747mg | Carbs 132.4g | Fiber 42.1g | Sugar 11.5g | Protein 65.7g

Lime Glazed Tofu

Servings: 6
Cooking Time: 14 Minutes

Ingredients:

- ⅔ cup coconut aminos
- 2 (14-oz) packages extra-firm, water-packed tofu, drained
- 6 tablespoons toasted sesame oil
- ⅔ cup lime juice

Directions:

1. Pat dry the tofu bars and slice into half-inch cubes.
2. Toss all the remaining ingredients in a small bowl.
3. Marinate for 4 hours in the refrigerator. Drain off the excess water.
4. Divide the tofu cubes in the two crisper plates.
5. Return the crisper plates to the Ninja Foodi Dual Zone Air Fryer.
6. Choose the Air Fry mode for Zone 1 and set the temperature to 400 degrees F/ 200 degrees C and the time to 14 minutes.
7. Select the "MATCH" button to copy the settings for Zone 2.
8. Initiate cooking by pressing the START/STOP button.
9. Toss the tofu once cooked halfway through, then resume cooking. 10. Serve warm.

Breaded Summer Squash

Servings: 4
Cooking Time: 10 Minutes

Ingredients:

- 4 cups yellow summer squash, sliced
- 3 tablespoons olive oil
- ½ teaspoon salt
- ½ teaspoon pepper
- ⅛ teaspoon cayenne pepper
- ¾ cup panko bread crumbs
- ¾ cup grated Parmesan cheese

Directions:

1. Mix crumbs, cheese, cayenne pepper, black pepper, salt and oil in a bowl.
2. Coat the squash slices with the breadcrumb mixture.
3. Place these slices in the air fryer baskets.
4. Return the air fryer basket 1 to Zone 1, and basket 2 to Zone 2 of the Ninja Foodi 2-Basket Air Fryer.
5. Choose the "Air Fry" mode for Zone 1 at 350 degrees F and 10 minutes of cooking time.
6. Select the "MATCH COOK" option to copy the settings for Zone 2.
7. Initiate cooking by pressing the START/PAUSE BUTTON.
8. Flip the squash slices once cooked half way through.
9. Serve warm.

Nutrition:

- (Per serving) Calories 193 | Fat 1g |Sodium 395mg | Carbs 38.7g | Fiber 1.6g | Sugar 0.9g | Protein 6.6g

Beets With Orange Gremolata And Goat's Cheese

Servings: 12
Cooking Time: 45 Minutes

Ingredients:

- 3 medium fresh golden beets (about 1 pound)
- 3 medium fresh beets (about 1 pound)
- 2 tablespoons lime juice
- 2 tablespoons orange juice
- ½ teaspoon fine sea salt
- 1 tablespoon minced fresh parsley
- 1 tablespoon minced fresh sage
- 1 garlic clove, minced
- 1 teaspoon grated orange zest
- 3 tablespoons crumbled goat's cheese
- 2 tablespoons sunflower kernels

Directions:

1. Scrub the beets and trim the tops by 1 inch.
2. Place the beets on a double thickness of heavy-duty foil . Fold the foil around the beets, sealing tightly.
3. Place a crisper plate in both drawers. Put the beets in a single layer in each drawer. Insert the drawers into the unit.
4. Select zone 1, then AIR FRY, then set the temperature to 360 degrees F/ 180 degrees C with a 45-minute timer. To match zone 2 settings to zone 1, choose MATCH. To begin, select START/STOP.
5. Remove the beets from the drawers after the timer has finished. Peel, halve, and slice them when they're cool enough to handle. Place them in a serving bowl.
6. Toss in the lime juice, orange juice, and salt to coat. Sprinkle the beets with the parsley, sage, garlic, and orange zest. The sunflower kernels and goat's cheese go on top.

Broccoli, Squash, & Pepper

Servings: 4
Cooking Time: 12 Minutes

Ingredients:

- 175g broccoli florets
- 1 red bell pepper, diced
- 1 tbsp olive oil
- ½ tsp garlic powder
- ¼ onion, sliced
- 1 zucchini, sliced
- 2 yellow squash, sliced
- Pepper
- Salt

Directions:

1. In a bowl, toss veggies with oil, garlic powder, pepper, and salt.
2. Insert a crisper plate in the Ninja Foodi air fryer baskets.
3. Add the vegetable mixture in both baskets.
4. Select zone 1 then select "air fry" mode and set the temperature to 390 degrees F for 12 minutes. Press "match" to match zone 2 settings to zone 1. Press "start/stop" to begin. Stir halfway through.

Nutrition:

- (Per serving) Calories 75 | Fat 3.9g |Sodium 62mg | Carbs 9.6g | Fiber 2.8g | Sugar 4.8g | Protein 2.9g

Bacon Potato Patties

Servings: 2
Cooking Time: 15 Minutes

Ingredients:

- 1 egg
- 600g mashed potatoes
- 119g breadcrumbs
- 2 bacon slices, cooked & chopped
- 235g cheddar cheese, shredded
- 15g flour
- Pepper
- Salt

Directions:

1. In a bowl, mix mashed potatoes with remaining ingredients until well combined.
2. Make patties from potato mixture and place on a plate.
3. Place plate in the refrigerator for 10 minutes
4. Insert a crisper plate in the Ninja Foodi air fryer baskets.
5. Place the prepared patties in both baskets.
6. Select zone 1 then select "air fry" mode and set the temperature to 390 degrees F for 15 minutes. Press "match" to match zone 2 settings to zone 1. Press "start/stop" to begin. Turn halfway through.

Nutrition:

- (Per serving) Calories 702 | Fat 26.8g |Sodium 1405mg | Carbs 84.8g | Fiber 2.7g | Sugar 3.8g | Protein 30.5g

Rosemary Asparagus & Potatoes

Servings: 6
Cooking Time: 30 Minutes

Ingredients:

- 125g asparagus, trimmed & cut into pieces
- 2 tsp garlic powder
- 2 tbsp rosemary, chopped
- 30ml olive oil
- 679g baby potatoes, quartered
- ½ tsp red pepper flakes
- Pepper
- Salt

Directions:

1. Insert a crisper plate in the Ninja Foodi air fryer baskets.
2. Toss potatoes with 1 tablespoon of oil, pepper, and salt in a bowl until well coated.
3. Add potatoes into in zone 1 basket.
4. Toss asparagus with remaining oil, red pepper flakes, pepper, garlic powder, and rosemary in a mixing bowl.
5. Add asparagus into the zone 2 basket.
6. Select zone 1, then select "air fry" mode and set the temperature to 390 degrees F for 20 minutes. Select zone 2, then select "air fry" mode and set the temperature to 390 degrees F for 10 minutes. Press "match" mode, then press "start/stop" to begin.

Nutrition:

- (Per serving) Calories 121 | Fat 5g |Sodium 40mg | Carbs 17.1g | Fiber 4.2g | Sugar 1g | Protein 4g

Curly Fries

Servings: 6
Cooking Time: 20 Minutes
Ingredients:
- 2 spiralized zucchinis
- 1 cup flour
- 2 tablespoons paprika
- 1 teaspoon cayenne pepper
- 1 teaspoon garlic powder
- 1 teaspoon black pepper
- 1 teaspoon salt
- 2 eggs
- Olive oil or cooking spray

Directions:
1. Mix flour with paprika, cayenne pepper, garlic powder, black pepper, and salt in a bowl.
2. Beat eggs in another bowl and dip the zucchini in the eggs.
3. Coat the zucchini with the flour mixture and divide it into two crisper plates. 4. Spray the zucchini with cooking oil.
4. Return the crisper plate to the Ninja Foodi Dual Zone Air Fryer.
5. Choose the Air Fry mode for Zone 1 and set the temperature to 400 degrees F/ 200 degrees C and the time to 20 minutes.
6. Select the "MATCH" button to copy the settings for Zone 2.
7. Initiate cooking by pressing the START/STOP button.
8. Toss the zucchini once cooked halfway through, then resume cooking.
9. Serve warm.

Desserts Recipes
Jelly Donuts

Servings: 4
Cooking Time: 5 Minutes
Ingredients:
- 1 package Pillsbury Grands (Homestyle)
- ½ cup seedless raspberry jelly
- 1 tablespoon butter, melted
- ½ cup sugar

Directions:
1. Install a crisper plate in both drawers. Place half of the biscuits in the zone 1 drawer and half in zone 2's, then insert the drawers into the unit. You may need to cook in batches.
2. Select zone 1, select AIR FRY, set temperature to 390°F, and set time to 22 minutes. Select MATCH to match zone 2 settings to zone 1. Press the START/STOP button to begin cooking.
3. Place the sugar into a wide bowl with a flat bottom.
4. Baste all sides of the cooked biscuits with the melted butter and roll in the sugar to cover completely.
5. Using a long cake tip, pipe 1–2 tablespoons of raspberry jelly into each biscuit. You've now got raspberry-filled donuts!

Crustless Peanut Butter Cheesecake And Pumpkin Pudding With Vanilla Wafers

Servings: 6
Cooking Time: 17 Minutes

Ingredients:
- Crustless Peanut Butter Cheesecake:
- 110 g cream cheese, softened
- 2 tablespoons powdered sweetener
- 1 tablespoon all-natural, no-sugar-added peanut butter
- ½ teaspoon vanilla extract
- 1 large egg, whisked
- Pumpkin Pudding with Vanilla Wafers:
- 250 g canned no-salt-added pumpkin purée (not pumpkin pie filling)
- 50 g packed brown sugar
- 3 tablespoons plain flour
- 1 egg, whisked
- 2 tablespoons milk
- 1 tablespoon unsalted butter, melted
- 1 teaspoon pure vanilla extract
- 4 low-fat vanilla, or plain wafers, crumbled
- Nonstick cooking spray

Directions:
1. Make the Crustless Peanut Butter Cheesecake :
2. In a medium bowl, mix cream cheese and sweetener until smooth. Add peanut butter and vanilla, mixing until smooth. Add egg and stir just until combined.
3. Spoon mixture into an ungreased springform pan and place into the zone 1 air fryer drawer. Adjust the temperature to 148ºC and bake for 10 minutes. Edges will be firm, but center will be mostly set with only a small amount of jiggle when done.
4. Let pan cool at room temperature 30 minutes, cover with plastic wrap, then place into refrigerator at least 2 hours. Serve chilled.
5. Make the Pumpkin Pudding with Vanilla Wafers :
6. Preheat the air fryer to 176ºC. Coat a baking pan with nonstick cooking spray. Set aside.
7. Mix the pumpkin purée, brown sugar, flour, whisked egg, milk, melted butter, and vanilla in a medium bowl and whisk to combine. Transfer the mixture to the baking pan.
8. Place the baking pan in the zone 2 air fryer drawer and bake for 12 to 17 minutes until set.
9. Remove the pudding from the drawer to a wire rack to cool.
10. Divide the pudding into four bowls and serve with the vanilla wafers sprinkled on top.

Apple Crisp

Servings: 8
Cooking Time: 15 Minutes

Ingredients:
- 3 cups apples, chopped
- 1 tablespoon pure maple syrup
- 2 teaspoons lemon juice
- 3 tablespoons all-purpose flour
- ⅓ cup quick oats
- ¼ cup brown sugar
- 2 tablespoons light butter, melted
- ½ teaspoon cinnamon

Directions:
1. Toss the chopped apples with 1 tablespoon of all-purpose flour, cinnamon, maple syrup, and lemon juice in a suitable bowl.
2. Divide the apples in the two air fryer baskets with their crisper plates.
3. Whisk oats, brown sugar, and remaining all-purpose flour in a small bowl.
4. Stir in melted butter, then divide this mixture over the apples.
5. Return the crisper plate to the Ninja Foodi Dual Zone Air Fryer.
6. Select the Bake mode for Zone 1 and set the temperature to 375 degrees F and the time to 14 minutes.
7. Select the "MATCH" button to copy the settings for Zone 2.
8. Initiate cooking by pressing the START/STOP button.
9. Enjoy fresh.

Mini Blueberry Pies

Servings: 2
Cooking Time: 15 Minutes

Ingredients:
- 1 box store-bought pie dough, Trader Joe's
- ¼ cup blueberry jam
- 1 teaspoon lemon zest
- 1 egg white, for brushing

Directions:
1. Take the store-bought pie dough and cut it into 3-inch circles.
2. Brush the dough with egg white all around the edges.
3. Now add blueberry jam and zest in the middle and top it with another circle.
4. Press the edges with a fork to seal it.
5. Make a slit in the middle of each pie and divide them between the baskets.
6. Set zone 1 to AIR FRY mode 360 degrees for 10 minutes.
7. Select the MATCH button for zone 2.
8. Once cooked, serve.

Pineapple Wontons

Servings: 5
Cooking Time: 15 To 18 Minutes

Ingredients:
- 225 g cream cheese
- 170 g finely chopped fresh pineapple
- 20 wonton wrappers
- Cooking oil spray

Directions:
1. In a small microwave-safe bowl, heat the cream cheese in the microwave on high power for 20 seconds to soften.
2. In a medium bowl, stir together the cream cheese and pineapple until mixed well.
3. Lay out the wonton wrappers on a work surface. A clean table or large cutting board works well.
4. Spoon 1½ teaspoons of the cream cheese mixture onto each wrapper. Be careful not to overfill.
5. Fold each wrapper diagonally across to form a triangle. Bring the 2 bottom corners up toward each other. Do not close the wrapper yet. Bring up the 2 open sides and push out any air. Squeeze the open edges together to seal.
6. Preheat the air fryer to 200°C.
7. Place the wontons into the two drawers. Spray the wontons with the cooking oil.
8. Cook wontons for 10 minutes, then remove the drawers, flip each wonton, and spray them with more oil. Reinsert the drawers to resume cooking for 5 to 8 minutes more until the wontons are light golden brown and crisp.
9. When the cooking is complete, cool for 5 minutes before serving.

Sweet Potato Donut Holes

Servings: 18 Donut Holes
Cooking Time: 4 To 5 Minutes

Ingredients:
- 125 g plain flour
- 65 g granulated sugar
- ¼ teaspoon baking soda
- 1 teaspoon baking powder
- ⅛ teaspoon salt
- 125 g cooked & mashed purple sweet potatoes
- 1 egg, beaten
- 2 tablespoons butter, melted
- 1 teaspoon pure vanilla extract
- Coconut, or avocado oil for misting or cooking spray

Directions:
1. Preheat the air fryer to 200°C.
2. In a large bowl, stir together the flour, sugar, baking soda, baking powder, and salt.
3. In a separate bowl, combine the potatoes, egg, butter, and vanilla and mix well.
4. Add potato mixture to dry ingredients and stir into a soft dough.
5. Shape dough into 1½-inch balls. Mist lightly with oil or cooking spray.
6. Place the donut holes in the two air fryer baskets, leaving a little space in between. Cook for 4 to 5 minutes, until done in center and lightly browned outside.

Pumpkin Muffins

Servings:4
Cooking Time:20

Ingredients:
- 1 and ½ cups of all-purpose flour
- ½ teaspoon baking soda
- ½ teaspoon of baking powder
- 1 and 1/4 teaspoons cinnamon, groaned
- 1/4 teaspoon ground nutmeg, grated
- 2 large eggs
- Salt, pinch
- 3/4 cup granulated sugar
- 1/2 cup dark brown sugar
- 1 and 1/2 cups of pumpkin puree
- 1/4 cup coconut milk

Directions:
1. Take 4 ramekins that are the size of a cup and layer them with muffin papers.
2. Crack an egg in a bowl and add brown sugar, baking soda, baking powder, cinnamon, nutmeg, and sugar.
3. Whisk it all very well with an electric hand beater.
4. Now, in a second bowl, mix the flour, and salt.
5. Now, mix the dry ingredients slowly with the wet ingredients.
6. Now, at the end fold in the pumpkin puree and milk, mix it well
7. Divide this batter into 4 ramekins.
8. Now, divide ramekins between both zones.
9. Set the time for zone 1 to 18 minutes at 360 degrees Fat AIRFRY mode.
10. Select the MATCH button for the zone 2 basket.
11. Check if not done, and let it AIR FRY for one more minute.
12. Once it is done, serve.

Nutrition:
- (Per serving) Calories 291| Fat6.4 g| Sodium 241mg | Carbs 57.1g | Fiber 4.4g | Sugar42 g | Protein 5.9g

Victoria Sponge Cake

Servings: 8
Cooking Time: 16 Minutes

Ingredients:
- Sponge Cake Ingredients
- 400g self-rising flour
- 450g caster sugar
- 50g lemon curd
- 200g butter
- 4 medium eggs
- 1 tablespoon vanilla essence
- 480ml skimmed milk
- 1 tablespoon olive oil
- 4 tablespoons strawberry jam
- Strawberry buttercream
- 115g butter
- 210g icing sugar
- ½ teaspoon strawberry food coloring
- 1 tablespoon single cream
- 1 teaspoon vanilla essence
- 1 teaspoon maple syrup

Directions:
1. Mix sugar and butter in a bowl using a hand mixer.
2. Beat eggs with oil, and vanilla in a bowl with the mixer until creamy.
3. Stir in milk, flour and curd then mix well.
4. Add butter mixture then mix well.
5. Divide this mixture in two 4 inches greased cake pans.
6. Place one pan in each air fryer basket.
7. Return the air fryer basket 1 to Zone 1, and basket 2 to Zone 2 of the Ninja Foodi 2-Basket Air Fryer.
8. Choose the "Air Fry" mode for Zone 1 and set the temperature to 375 degrees F and 16 minutes of cooking time.
9. Select the "MATCH COOK" option to copy the settings for Zone 2.
10. Initiate cooking by pressing the START/PAUSE BUTTON.
11. Meanwhile, blend the buttercream ingredients in a mixer until fluffy.
12. Place one cake on a plate and top it with the buttercream.
13. Top it jam and then with the other cake.
14. Serve.

Nutrition:
- (Per serving) Calories 284 | Fat 16g | Sodium 252mg | Carbs 31.6g | Fiber 0.9g | Sugar 6.6g | Protein 3.7g

Olive Oil Cake & Old-fashioned Fudge Pie

Servings: 16
Cooking Time: 30 Minutes

Ingredients:
- Olive Oil Cake:
- 120 g blanched finely ground almond flour
- 5 large eggs, whisked
- 175 ml extra-virgin olive oil
- 75 g granulated sweetener
- 1 teaspoon vanilla extract
- 1 teaspoon baking powder
- Old-Fashioned Fudge Pie:
- 300 g granulated sugar
- 40 g unsweetened cocoa powder
- 70 g self-raising flour
- 3 large eggs, unbeaten
- 12 tablespoons unsalted butter, melted
- 1½ teaspoons vanilla extract
- 1 (9-inch) unbaked piecrust
- 30 g icing sugar (optional)

Directions:
1. Make the Olive Oil Cake :
2. In a large bowl, mix all ingredients. Pour batter into an ungreased round nonstick baking dish.
3. Place dish into the zone 1 air fryer basket. Adjust the temperature to 150°C and bake for 30 minutes. The cake will be golden on top and firm in the center when done.
4. Let cake cool in dish 30 minutes before slicing and serving.
5. Make the Old-Fashioned Fudge Pie :
6. In a medium bowl, stir together the sugar, cocoa powder, and flour. Stir in the eggs and melted butter. Stir in the vanilla.
7. Preheat the air fryer to 175°C.
8. Pour the chocolate filing into the crust.
9. Cook in the zone 2 basket for 25 to 30 minutes, stirring every 10 minutes, until a knife inserted into the middle comes out clean. Let sit for 5 minutes before dusting with icing sugar to serve.

Molten Chocolate Almond Cakes

Servings: 3
Cooking Time: 13 Minutes

Ingredients:

- Butter and flour for the ramekins
- 110 g bittersweet chocolate, chopped
- 110 g unsalted butter
- 2 eggs
- 2 egg yolks
- 50 g granulated sugar
- ½ teaspoon pure vanilla extract, or almond extract
- 1 tablespoon plain flour
- 3 tablespoons ground almonds
- 8 to 12 semisweet chocolate discs (or 4 chunks of chocolate)
- Cocoa powder or icing sugar, for dusting
- Toasted almonds, coarsely chopped

Directions:

1. Butter and flour three ramekins.
2. Melt the chocolate and butter together, either in the microwave or in a double boiler. In a separate bowl, beat the eggs, egg yolks and sugar together until light and smooth. Add the vanilla extract. Whisk the chocolate mixture into the egg mixture. Stir in the flour and ground almonds.
3. Preheat the air fryer to 165°C.
4. Transfer the batter carefully to the buttered ramekins, filling halfway. Place two or three chocolate discs in the center of the batter and then fill the ramekins to ½-inch below the top with the remaining batter. Place the ramekins into the zone 1 air fryer basket and air fry for 13 minutes. The sides of the cake should be set, but the centers should be slightly soft. Remove the ramekins from the air fryer and let the cakes sit for 5 minutes.
5. Run a butter knife around the edge of the ramekins and invert the cakes onto a plate. Lift the ramekin off the plate slowly and carefully so that the cake doesn't break. Dust with cocoa powder or icing sugar and serve with a scoop of ice cream and some coarsely chopped toasted almonds.

Pecan And Cherry Stuffed Apples

Servings: 4
Cooking Time: 20 Minutes

Ingredients:

- 4 apples (about 565 g)
- 40 g chopped pecans
- 50 g dried tart cherries
- 1 tablespoon melted butter
- 3 tablespoons brown sugar
- ¼ teaspoon allspice
- Pinch salt
- Ice cream, for serving

Directions:

1. Cut off top ½ inch from each apple; reserve tops. With a melon baller, core through stem ends without breaking through the bottom.
2. Preheat the air fryer to 175°C. Combine pecans, cherries, butter, brown sugar, allspice, and a pinch of salt. Stuff mixture into the hollow centers of the apples. Cover with apple tops. Put in the air fryer basket, using tongs. Air fry for 20 to 25 minutes, or just until tender.
3. Serve warm with ice cream.

Grilled Peaches

Servings: 4
Cooking Time: 10 Minutes
Ingredients:
- 2 yellow peaches
- ¼ cup graham cracker crumbs
- ¼ cup brown sugar
- ¼ cup butter, diced into tiny cubes
- Whipped cream or ice cream, for serving.

Directions:
1. Cut the peaches into wedges and pull out their pits.
2. Install a crisper plate in both drawers. Put half of the peach wedges into the drawer in zone 1 and half in zone 2's. Sprinkle the tops of the wedges with the crumbs, sugar, and butter. Insert the drawers into the unit.
3. Select zone 1, select AIR FRY, set the temperature to 390°F, and set the time to 10 minutes. Select MATCH to match zone 2 settings to zone 1. Press the START/STOP button to begin cooking.

Brownies Muffins

Servings: 3
Cooking Time: 10 Minutes
Ingredients:
- ¼ egg
- ⅛ cup walnuts, chopped
- 1 tablespoon vegetable oil
- ¼ package fudge brownie mix
- ½ teaspoon water

Directions:
1. Take a bowl, add all the ingredients. Mix well.
2. Place the mixture into prepared muffin molds evenly.
3. Line each basket of "Zone 1" and "Zone 2" with parchment paper.
4. Press "Zone 1" and "Zone 2" and then rotate the knob for each zone to select "Air Fry".
5. Set the temperature to 300 degrees F/ 150 degrees C for both zones and then set the time for 5 minutes to preheat.
6. After preheating, arrange the muffin molds into the basket of each zone.
7. Slide each basket into Air Fryer and set the time for 10 minutes.
8. After cooking time is completed, remove from Air Fryer.
9. Refrigerate.
10. Serve and enjoy!

Moist Chocolate Espresso Muffins

Servings: 8
Cooking Time: 18 Minutes

Ingredients:

- 1 egg
- 177ml milk
- ½ tsp baking soda
- ½ tsp espresso powder
- ½ tsp baking powder
- 50g cocoa powder
- 78ml vegetable oil
- 1 tsp apple cider vinegar
- 1 tsp vanilla
- 150g brown sugar
- 150g all-purpose flour
- ½ tsp salt

Directions:

1. In a bowl, whisk egg, vinegar, oil, brown sugar, vanilla, and milk.
2. Add flour, cocoa powder, baking soda, baking powder, espresso powder, and salt and stir until well combined.
3. Pour batter into the silicone muffin moulds.
4. Insert a crisper plate in Ninja Foodi air fryer baskets.
5. Place muffin moulds in both baskets.
6. Select zone 1 then select "bake" mode and set the temperature to 320 degrees F for 18 minutes. Press match cook to match zone 2 settings to zone 1. Press "start/stop" to begin.

Nutrition:

- (Per serving) Calories 222 | Fat 11g | Sodium 251mg | Carbs 29.6g | Fiber 2g | Sugar 14.5g | Protein 4g

Zucchini Bread

Servings: 12
Cooking Time: 40 Minutes

Ingredients:

- 220 g coconut flour
- 2 teaspoons baking powder
- 150 g granulated sweetener
- 120 ml coconut oil, melted
- 1 teaspoon apple cider vinegar
- 1 teaspoon vanilla extract
- 3 eggs, beaten
- 1 courgette, grated
- 1 teaspoon ground cinnamon

Directions:

1. In the mixing bowl, mix coconut flour with baking powder, sweetener, coconut oil, apple cider vinegar, vanilla extract, eggs, courgette, and ground cinnamon.
2. Transfer the mixture into the two air fryer drawers and flatten it in the shape of the bread.
3. Cook the bread at 176ºC for 40 minutes.

Gluten-free Spice Cookies

Servings: 4
Cooking Time: 12 Minutes

Ingredients:

- 4 tablespoons unsalted butter, at room temperature
- 2 tablespoons agave nectar
- 1 large egg
- 2 tablespoons water
- 240 g almond flour
- 100 g granulated sugar
- 2 teaspoons ground ginger
- 1 teaspoon ground cinnamon
- ½ teaspoon freshly grated nutmeg
- 1 teaspoon baking soda
- ¼ teaspoon kosher, or coarse sea salt

Directions:

1. Line the bottom of the air fryer basket with baking paper cut to fit.
2. In a large bowl, using a hand mixer, beat together the butter, agave, egg, and water on medium speed until light and fluffy.
3. Add the almond flour, sugar, ginger, cinnamon, nutmeg, baking soda, and salt. Beat on low speed until well combined.
4. Roll the dough into 2-tablespoon balls and arrange them on the baking paper in the basket. Set the air fryer to 165ºC, and cook for 12 minutes, or until the tops of cookies are lightly browned.
5. Transfer to a wire rack and let cool completely. Store in an airtight container for up to a week.

Cinnamon Bread Twists

Servings: 4
Cooking Time: 15 Minutes

Ingredients:

- Bread Twists Dough
- 120g all-purpose flour
- 1 teaspoon baking powder
- ¼ teaspoon salt
- 150g fat free Greek yogurt
- Brushing
- 2 tablespoons light butter
- 2 tablespoons granulated sugar
- 1-2 teaspoons ground cinnamon, to taste

Directions:

1. Mix flour, salt and baking powder in a bowl.
2. Stir in yogurt and the rest of the dough ingredients in a bowl.
3. Mix well and make 8 inches long strips out of this dough.
4. Twist the strips and place them in the air fryer baskets.
5. Return the air fryer basket 1 to Zone 1, and basket 2 to Zone 2 of the Ninja Foodi 2-Basket Air Fryer.
6. Choose the "Air Fry" mode for Zone 1 at 375 degrees F and 15 minutes of cooking time.
7. Select the "MATCH COOK" option to copy the settings for Zone 2.
8. Initiate cooking by pressing the START/PAUSE BUTTON.
9. Flip the twists once cooked halfway through.
10. Mix butter with cinnamon and sugar in a bowl.
11. Brush this mixture over the twists.
12. Serve.

Nutrition:

- (Per serving) Calories 391 | Fat 24g | Sodium 142mg | Carbs 38.5g | Fiber 3.5g | Sugar 21g | Protein 6.6g

Cream Cheese Shortbread Cookies

Servings: 12 Cookies
Cooking Time: 20 Minutes

Ingredients:

- 60 ml coconut oil, melted
- 55 g cream cheese, softened
- 100 g granulated sweetener
- 1 large egg, whisked
- 190 g blanched finely ground almond flour
- 1 teaspoon almond extract

Directions:

1. Combine all ingredients in a large bowl to form a firm ball.
2. Place dough on a sheet of plastic wrap and roll into a 12-inch-long log shape. Roll log in plastic wrap and place in refrigerator 30 minutes to chill.
3. Remove log from plastic and slice into twelve equal cookies. Cut two sheets of baking paper to fit the two air fryer baskets. Place the cookies on the two ungreased sheet and put into the two air fryer baskets. Adjust the temperature to 160°C and bake for 10 minutes, turning cookies halfway through cooking. They will be lightly golden when done.
4. Let cool 15 minutes before serving to avoid crumbling.

Coconut-custard Pie And Pecan Brownies

Servings: 9
Cooking Time: 20 To 23 Minutes

Ingredients:

- Coconut-Custard Pie:
- 240 ml milk
- 50 g granulated sugar, plus 2 tablespoons
- 30 g scone mix
- 1 teaspoon vanilla extract
- 2 eggs
- 2 tablespoons melted butter
- Cooking spray
- 50 g desiccated, sweetened coconut
- Pecan Brownies:
- 50 g blanched finely ground almond flour
- 55 g powdered sweetener
- 2 tablespoons unsweetened cocoa powder
- ½ teaspoon baking powder
- 55 g unsalted butter, softened
- 1 large egg
- 35 g chopped pecans
- 40 g low-carb, sugar-free chocolate chips

Directions:

1. Make the Coconut-Custard Pie :
2. Place all ingredients except coconut in a medium bowl.
3. Using a hand mixer, beat on high speed for 3 minutes.
4. Let sit for 5 minutes.
5. Preheat the air fryer to 164°C.
6. Spray a baking pan with cooking spray and place pan in the zone 1 air fryer drawer.
7. Pour filling into pan and sprinkle coconut over top.
8. Cook pie for 20 to 23 minutes or until center sets.
9. Make the Pecan Brownies :
10. In a large bowl, mix almond flour, sweetener, cocoa powder, and baking powder. Stir in butter and egg. 2. Fold in pecans and chocolate chips. Scoop mixture into a round baking pan. Place pan into the zone 2 air fryer drawer. 3. Adjust the temperature to 148°C and bake for 20 minutes. 4. When fully cooked a toothpick inserted in center will come out clean. Allow 20 minutes to fully cool and firm up.

Simple Pineapple Sticks And Crispy Pineapple Rings

Servings: 9
Cooking Time: 10 Minutes

Ingredients:
- Simple Pineapple Sticks:
- ½ fresh pineapple, cut into sticks
- 25 g desiccated coconut
- Crispy Pineapple Rings:
- 240 ml rice milk
- 85 g plain flour
- 120 ml water
- 25 g unsweetened flaked coconut
- 4 tablespoons granulated sugar
- ½ teaspoon baking soda
- ½ teaspoon baking powder
- ½ teaspoon vanilla essence
- ½ teaspoon ground cinnamon
- ¼ teaspoon ground star anise
- Pinch of kosher, or coarse sea salt
- 1 medium pineapple, peeled and sliced

Directions:
1. Simple Pineapple Sticks :
2. Preheat the air fryer to 204ºC.
3. Coat the pineapple sticks in the desiccated coconut and put in the zone 1 air fryer drawer.
4. Air fry for 10 minutes.
5. Serve immediately
6. Crispy Pineapple Rings :
7. Preheat the air fryer to 204ºC.
8. In a large bowl, stir together all the ingredients except the pineapple.
9. Dip each pineapple slice into the batter until evenly coated.
10. Arrange the pineapple slices in the zone 2 drawer and air fry for 6 to 8 minutes until golden brown.
11. Remove from the drawer to a plate and cool for 5 minutes before serving warm

Apple Wedges With Apricots And Coconut Mixed Berry Crisp

Servings: 10
Cooking Time: 20 Minutes

Ingredients:
- Apple Wedges with Apricots:
- 4 large apples, peeled and sliced into 8 wedges
- 2 tablespoons light olive oil
- 95 g dried apricots, chopped
- 1 to 2 tablespoons granulated sugar
- ½ teaspoon ground cinnamon
- Coconut Mixed Berry Crisp:
- 1 tablespoon butter, melted
- 340 g mixed berries
- 65 g granulated sweetener
- 1 teaspoon pure vanilla extract
- ½ teaspoon ground cinnamon
- ¼ teaspoon ground cloves
- ¼ teaspoon grated nutmeg
- 50 g coconut chips, for garnish

Directions:
1. Make the Apple Wedges with Apricots :
2. Preheat the zone 1 air fryer drawer to 180°C.
3. Toss the apple wedges with the olive oil in a mixing bowl until well coated.
4. Place the apple wedges in the zone 1 air fryer drawer and air fry for 12 to 15 minutes.
5. Sprinkle with the dried apricots and air fry for another 3 minutes.
6. Meanwhile, thoroughly combine the sugar and cinnamon in a small bowl.
7. Remove the apple wedges from the drawer to a plate. Serve sprinkled with the sugar mixture.
8. Make the Coconut Mixed Berry Crisp :
9. Preheat the zone 2 air fryer drawer to 164°C. Coat a baking pan with melted butter.
10. Put the remaining ingredients except the coconut chips in the prepared baking pan.
11. Bake in the preheated air fryer for 20 minutes.
12. Serve garnished with the coconut chips.

Recipe Index

A

Apple Crisp 90

Apple Wedges With Apricots And Coconut Mixed Berry Crisp 101

Asparagus And Bell Pepper Strata And Greek Bagels 14

Asian Chicken 51

Asian Glazed Meatballs 55

Asian Pork Skewers 57

Air Fried Chicken Legs 40

Air Fried Pot Stickers 38

Air-fried Tofu Cutlets With Cacio E Pepe Brussels Sprouts 77

B

Bbq Corn 81

Blueberry Coffee Cake And Maple Sausage Patties 20

Blackened Red Snapper 66

Breaded Summer Squash 85

Breakfast Cheese Sandwich 19

Breakfast Meatballs 15

Breakfast Sammies 13

Breakfast Sausage And Cauliflower 17

Broccoli And Cheese Stuffed Chicken 41

Broccoli, Squash, & Pepper 86

Brownies Muffins 96

Buffalo Seitan With Crispy Zucchini Noodles 78

Buttermilk Fried Chicken 43

Bacon Potato Patties 87

Bacon And Egg Omelet 12

Baked Peach Oatmeal 18

Balsamic Vegetables 82

Balsamic-glazed Tofu With Roasted Butternut Squash 80

Barbecue Chicken Drumsticks With Crispy Kale Chips 39

Bell Peppers With Sausages 55

Beef Jerky Pineapple Jerky 38

Beef Kofta Kebab 59

Beets With Orange Gremolata And Goat's Cheese 86

C

Cheddar Quiche 35

Cheesy Baked Eggs 22

Chicken Crescent Wraps 34

Chicken Kebabs 45

Chicken Ranch Wraps 51

Chicken With Pineapple And Peach 43

Chicken And Ham Meatballs With Dijon Sauce 41

Chicken Stuffed Mushrooms 25

Chilean Sea Bass With Olive Relish And Snapper With Tomato 65

Chili Chicken Wings 50

Crunchy Basil White Beans And Artichoke And Olive Pitta Flatbread 28

Crustless Peanut Butter Cheesecake And Pumpkin Pudding With Vanilla Wafers 89

Crab Rangoon Dip With Crispy Wonton Strips 30

Cream Cheese Shortbread Cookies 99

Crisp Paprika Chicken Drumsticks And Chicken Breasts With Asparagus And Beans 46

Crispy Calamari Rings 29

Crispy Fried Quail 40

Crispy Ranch Nuggets 48

Crispy Sesame Chicken 44

Curly Fries 88

Cilantro Lime Steak 54

Cinnamon Bread Twists 98

Cinnamon-raisin Bagels Everything Bagels 16

Coconut Cream Mackerel 70

Coconut-custard Pie And Pecan Brownies 99

Codfish With Herb Vinaigrette 68

E

Egg In Bread Hole 19

Easy Chicken Thighs 50

F

Flavorful Salmon With Green Beans 67

French Toasts 15

Fresh Mix Veggies In Air Fryer 83

Fried Pickles 27

Five-spice Pork Belly 58

Fish Tacos 72

G

Gluten-free Spice Cookies 98

Grill Cheese Sandwich 27

Grilled Peaches 96

Garlic Bread 36

Garlic Butter Steaks 58

Garlic Dill Wings 42

Garlic Herbed Baked Potatoes 82

Garlic Potato Wedges In Air Fryer 83

Garlic-rosemary Brussels Sprouts 81

Goat Cheese And Garlic Crostini & Sweet Bacon Potato Crunchies 24

H

Honey Glazed Bbq Pork Ribs 57

Honey Pecan Shrimp 75

Honey Teriyaki Salmon 76

I

Italian Baked Cod 73

Italian Sausage And Cheese Meatballs 61

Italian Sausages With Peppers And Teriyaki Rump Steak With Broccoli 56

Italian-style Meatballs With Garlicky Roasted Broccoli 60

J

Jalapeño Popper Dip With Tortilla Chips 32

Jalapeño Poppers And Greek Potato Skins With Olives And Feta 37

Jelly Donuts 88

Jelly Doughnuts 11

K

Kielbasa And Cabbage 54

L

Lemon Pepper Salmon With Asparagus 70

Lemon-pepper Chicken Thighs With Buttery Roasted Radishes 47

Lemony Prawns And Courgette 63

Lime Glazed Tofu 85

M

Mushroom Roll-ups 76

Mushroom Rolls 31

Marinated Ginger Garlic Salmon 66

Marinated Steak & Mushrooms 52

Mini Blueberry Pies 90

Molten Chocolate Almond Cakes 95

Morning Patties 11

Mozzarella Stuffed Beef And Pork Meatballs 59

Moist Chocolate Espresso Muffins 97

O

Olive Oil Cake & Old-fashioned Fudge Pie 94

Onion Pakoras 34

Onion Omelette And Buffalo Egg Cups 23

Orange-mustard Glazed Salmon And Cucumber And Salmon Salad 69

P

Prawns Curry 75

Pretzels 33

Puff Pastry 22

Pumpkin Muffins 92

Pecan And Cherry Stuffed Apples 95

Pecan-crusted Chicken Tenders 39

Pepper Poppers 84

Pepperoni Pizza Dip 36

Pineapple Wontons 91

Potatoes Lyonnaise 18

Q

Quick And Easy Blueberry Muffins 17

Quinoa Patties 79

R

Rosemary Asparagus & Potatoes 87

S

Scallops And Spinach With Cream Sauce And Confetti Salmon Burgers 74

Short Ribs & Root Vegetables 63

Spicy Chicken Wings 45

Spicy Chicken Sandwiches With "fried" Pickles 49

Stuffed Bell Peppers 26

Steak Fajitas With Onions And Peppers 53

Steamed Cod With Garlic And Swiss Chard 73

Sweet Potato Donut Holes 91

Salmon Fritters With Courgette & Cajun And Lemon Pepper Cod 71

Salmon Patties 64

Salmon With Broccoli And Cheese 68

Sausage With Eggs 21

Savory Soufflé 21

Seasoned Tuna Steaks 67

Simple Lamb Meatballs 53

Simple Pineapple Sticks And Crispy Pineapple Rings 100

T

Turkey And Beef Meatballs 62

Taco Seasoned Steak 61

Teriyaki Chicken Skewers 42

V

Veggie Shrimp Toast 26

Victoria Sponge Cake 93

W

Wholemeal Blueberry Muffins 12

Waffle Fries 35

Y

Yogurt Lamb Chops 52

Z

Zucchini Bread 97

Zucchini With Stuffing 84

Printed in Great Britain
by Amazon